Boys Gone Wild

Fame, Fortune, and Deviance among Professional Football Players

Eric M. Carter

University Press of America,® Inc.
Lanham · Boulder · New York · Toronto · Plymouth, UK

Copyright © 2009 by
University Press of America,® Inc.
4501 Forbes Boulevard
Suite 200
Lanham, Maryland 20706
UPA Acquisitions Department (301) 459-3366

Estover Road
Plymouth PL6 7PY
United Kingdom

All rights reserved
Printed in the United States of America
British Library Cataloging in Publication Information Available

Library of Congress Control Number: 2009924599
ISBN-13: 978-0-7618-4655-0 (paperback : alk. paper)
eISBN-13: 978-0-7618-4656-7

™ The paper used in this publication meets the minimum
requirements of American National Standard for Information
Sciences—Permanence of Paper for Printed Library Materials,
ANSI Z39.48-1992

Contents

Preface		v
Acknowledgements		vii
Chapter One	Introduction: Consequences of America's Obsession	1
Chapter Two	It's Lonely (Anomie) at the Top: Theoretical Interpretations of Deviant Behavior	9
Chapter Three	Accessing the Lives of Professional Football Players: Stories Revealed	35
Chapter Four	Illegal Procedure: Seeing Patterns of Deviance	45
Chapter Five	Out of Bounds: Seeing Patterns of Anomie	55
Chapter Six	Inside the Huddle: Patterns of Social Support and Ties	61
Chapter Seven	Moving the Chains: From Observation to Quantification	73
Chapter Eight	The Final Score: What the Numbers Mean	93
Chapter Nine	Key Considerations for the Future: Social Control or Empowerment?	113
Index		125
About the Author		131

Preface

"Let me tell you about life in the NFL. N stands for 'not.' F stands for 'for.' And L stands for 'long.' . . . Lifestyle in the NFL, if you're not careful, if you're not rooted and grounded, and you know who you are, it can consume you," one NFL player told me. He went on to tell me that many NFL players get wild and crazy, act with abandon, become "bad boys." Another NFL player revealed, "I've slept with hundreds of women, snorted coke 'til my nose bled, you name it, I've done it. . . . I thought I was fucking superman. . . . Anything I wanted, I just snapped my fingers . . . but let me tell you, it didn't take long for me to realize how miserable I was, I hated myself." So, why would professional athletes, who have wealth, status, fame, and women, commit violent acts, abuse alcohol and drugs, be depressed and unhappy, and even in some cases be suicidal? There have been at least 385 serious offences that have resulted in arrests of NFL players since January, 2000 (Schrotenboer 2008). Research conducted by Jeff Benedict and Don Yaeger (1998) showed that one out of five NFL players has been charged with serious crimes. And according to my recent research, nearly 35% of NFL players have been arrested after their entrance into the professional ranks. What explains their wild, deviant behavior? Why *are* so many players failing at success? My argument is that the sudden wealth and fame acquired by NFL players not only contributes to, but is a key factor involved in, off-the-field player deviance and unlawful behavior.

The core problem of the research I conducted for this book is the issue of the behavioral outcomes of NFL players who are suddenly wealthy and what negative consequences this can have for them. The nearly immediate wealth and star-power these athletes experience at the signing of their first professional contract can have many unintended, and at times, devastating consequences, as the rapid change in their lives leaves many of them without the normal moorings that society offers. This is exactly the meaning of *anomie*, the key theoretical construct of this research.

The significance of this situation for these players and their families creates a series of consequences which are quite unpredictable. The social environment of the players is foreign to most outsiders as well as most journalists and sportswriters. As Adam Gopnik (2007) from *The New Yorker* states, "The atmosphere is closed, guarded, and immensely knowing about the media" and others seeking any intimate information about players. "With the best will in the world there is very little you can squeeze out of the players that has not been pasteurized first by the agents and the league and the players' entourage, and by the players' understanding—essentially true—that the reporter is on nobody's side but his own" (38). Yet, I gained intimate access to 104 NFL players from 2001-2006. These players told me incredible stories of destructive lifestyles and deviant life-choices they lived or witnessed others live. Many said they were literally unable to cope with the freedom that came with sudden wealth and fame. In other words, here were millionaire athletes, who had everything most Americans only dream of, but couldn't stay out of trouble. When I asked one why he couldn't curb his illegal behavior, I'll never forget what he told me: "I was instantly rich, and I couldn't handle it." That was during my first in-depth conversation. As I heard this repeated over and over again, I realized it needed to be the theme of this book.

Eric M. Carter
Georgetown, Kentucky, USA
October 28, 2008

References

Benedict, Jeff, and Don Yaeger. 1998. *Pros and cons: The criminals who play in the NFL*. Boston: Warner Books.
Gopnik, Adam. 2007. "The unbeautiful game." *The New Yorker* 82: 38.
Schrotenboer, Brent. 2008. "NFL Crime." *Union Tribune*. http://www.signonsandiego.com/sports/nfl/20080419-9999-1s19nflrail1.html. Retrieved June 24, 2008.

Acknowledgments

I wish to thank Georgetown College for awarding me the Henlein Junior Faculty Research Fellowship. This fellowship was incredibly valuable in helping me write this book.

I want to extend a profound thank you to Dr. Michael Carter and Dr. Yolanda Gallardo-Carter. They have reviewed countless drafts of this book and have provided invaluable critique and assistance throughout this project.

I appreciate the work of a number of my undergraduate students who provided research assistance throughout this process. Particularly, I would like to thank Tara Campbell, Ryan Anderson, Demetrius Guions, Jerry Turner, Matt Walls, Cheyenne Moore, Donnovan Brown, Hollis Giles, Johonne Hamilton, and Vincent Crutcher.

Very special gratitude is extended to all of the professional football players willing to talk to me for this book. They generously offered their time and trusted me with their personal information and stories. I am truly grateful for their trust. This book would not have been possible without their unyielding participation.

To Donald White and Dorothy Albritton, for their assistance with editing and formatting, and to University Press of America, I say thanks as well.

I also say thanks to my parents, Mike and Debbie, who throughout the many phases of this project, were extremely supportive.

Last but certainly not least, a very special thank you to my wife Yoli, and my two children, Cris and Adriana. Their support has meant the world to me.

Chapter One

Introduction: Consequences of America's Obsession

> Professional football is the ultimate and *original* reality show and its participants are the "gladiators of modern culture . . . and with that comes the pluses and minuses associated with players who are larger than life." (Lowry 2003, 87)

This book is about the deviant lifestyles of professional football players. Other books have been written about the phenomenon of professional football and even troubled athletes. Yet, these books either fail to account for the many problems this phenomenon has caused for the athletes or they lack in-depth explanation concerning the relationship between athletes and deviance. Therefore, this isn't that book. This is a book that provides a theoretical and empirical explanation by addressing the key social factors that contribute to the deviant and illegal actions of professional football players.

The players represented in this book have much in common. As their stories unfolded, certain themes frequently surfaced. What they have in common is fame, fortune, and erratic behavior. These athletes serve as our heroes and as examples of successful social mobility. Yet, they also serve as social deviants and perpetuate negative societal stereotypes. This paradox is one that is often typical of the larger sphere of sport.

The Cultural Transformation of Athletes to Mythic Figures

To most Americans, the importance of sports, and professional sports in particular, in our national culture is obvious. More specifically, the industry of professional football has been one of the most successful growth industries in recent decades. Since 1960, when Commissioner Pete Rozelle helped marry professional football to television, the sport has had a profound impact on the popular imagination in American society. This has been due in no small part to the commodification of the sport and its subsequent packaging by the mass media, television in particular. At the core of my research is the issue of the behavior outcomes of players who are suddenly wealthy and famous, and what negative consequences this can have for them. This wealth and fame in the first place is based on a complex interplay of the sport's media popularity (and the advertising revenue that is thus generated) and its immense popularity as a cultural ritual for millions of fans.

Within this sociological framework, the religious overtones of football's popular appeal are also quite apparent. Emile Durkheim ([1912] 1965) stated that the old gods had died, and he contemplated the issue of which new gods would replace them. It does not seem to be stretching a point to suggest that professional sports have to a large degree taken over some of the original functions of religion in modern society. In this sense, American professional football has many of the characteristics of what Robert Bellah (1967) has called a "civil religion," with its rituals and its pantheon of mythic figures.

It's important to understand how all of these elements converge in making football such a significant component in popular culture. For many Americans, professional football provides a much-needed sense of community in our highly individualistic culture. The rituals and the passion associated with football in America cut across boundaries of age, race and ethnicity, gender, political affiliation, and many others to provide a feeling of unity in the face of so many cross-cutting conflicts within society. It is in this sense, and based on this profound need for a feeling of community, that professional football has emerged as a sort of pseudo-religion for millions of Americans.

The media help to perpetuate these beliefs and rituals. And, with their heavy emphasis on touting the material well-being of professional athletes, the media also help to ensure that fans of professional football are kept fully aware of the possibility of the "American Dream" of great wealth and prestige. Such emphasis helps to perpetuate the myth that even people from the humblest origins can reach the pinnacle of success as long as they simply work hard enough. By reinforcing such ideas, along with a related package of ideas promoting competition, masculinity, and individual achievement, the media have promoted football as a package of American virtues to be played out every fall on millions of television sets and computer screens across America, and increasingly the world.

In the process of promoting professional football in such a manner, the media has elevated the sport's top athletes into demi-gods and cult figures, who are then presumed to be role models for the youth of America, particularly those from underprivileged backgrounds for whom similar athletic prowess can be perceived as a "way out." The result of this for the athletes is sudden fortune, as they in turn make many more millions for their owners. But such rapid fame and fortunes can sometimes have devastating consequences for these young men, as the sudden change in their lives leaves many of them without a sense of what is normal. This is exactly the meaning of *anomie*, the core concept in this analysis of the negative effects of such sudden change on the lives of these athletes.

The media report on a regular basis the deviance of professional athletes, an ironic reporting of a problem that they have helped create. I would argue that the research conducted for this book is an important step in moving beyond facile interpretations of such deviant behavior to a more careful, systematic, and theoretically-grounded understanding of the larger circumstances that often lead to the kind of behavior that makes negative headlines. A fuller understanding of the context in which professional sports operates in our culture, with its religious overtones and media hype that, as one player told me, "makes gods out of twenty-one year olds," is a critical step in locating the source of such problems and helping to keep these young athletes grounded in reality (for further discussion of the emergence and importance of professional sports in American culture, see Coakley 2007; Eitzen 2005; Eitzen & Sage 2009; MacCambridge 2004; Sage 1998).

Overview of the Book

Boys Gone Wild is an attempt to contribute to the understanding of deviant and illegal behavior among professional athletes. At the core, this book takes an in-depth look at 104 current and former National Football League players regarding the effect of sudden economic change on their personal and professional lives. Most professional football players go from being a non-working college student to a highly paid, visible professional when they sign their first contract. For many people, this is a dream come true which should bring prosperity, wealth, and a lifetime of economic security. Yet, almost daily, the sports pages contain negative stories about the criminal activities or social behaviors of professional football players. According to Mark Starr and Allison Samuels (2000), "these athletes are crashing and burning in front of our eyes" (56). Troubled by this kind of deviant behavior, they observed:

> The recipe for trouble has always existed in professional sports: ill-prepared young kids ushered too quickly into the spotlight, bathed in adoration, showered with riches, surrounded by hangers-on. But the money and media attention has intensified the pace of it all. One pro athlete understands it well: "Things come at you so fast sometimes you don't know what to do. We're only human." (57)

If one can secure a better life through success in one's profession, then why do professional sports players experience different kinds of turmoil and trouble? More specifically, why is deviant behavior among many NFL players so common despite the prosperity and economic well-being available to them? Why do some players become law breakers and others law abiders? Are there identifiable characteristics that help players adapt to the pressures of professional football? Are there characteristics that encourage players to fall victim to deviant and, sometimes, illegal behavior?

The proponents of social control (Hirschi 1969), social support (Vaux 1988), and anomie (Durkheim ([1897] 1951; Merton 1938; Parsons 1937) theories have offered plausible explanations of social deviance. These theories come out of the sociological work of Emile Durkheim ([1893] 1933; [1897] 1951; [1925] 1961). Durkheim's classic study of suicide ([1897] 1951) first showed how diminished social ties contributed to the loss of clear social roles and norms.

Moreover, Durkheim ([1897] 1951) analyzed forms of deviant behavior brought about by social change and first introduced the theoretical and analytical term *anomie* into the study of sociology. In essence, anomie describes the impact of sudden economic change and the subsequent loss of social bonds on human beings. For this book, I rely on Durkheim's framework to ask the question of whether anomie exists among professional football players who have experienced sudden wealth. If so, does this result in deviance? And, what are the factors that contribute to anomic conditions and deviant or criminal behavior?

Importance of this Book

The deviant and sometimes criminal off-field behavior of NFL players has been the subject of much controversy. In most of American life, one might believe that wealth would bring happiness, satisfaction with life, and greater financial and even emotional stability. But, when many NFL players sign their first contract, their bank accounts become large, their egos become inflated, and they begin to turn their lives upside down. Instead of increasing satisfaction and stability, wealth and fame often increase deviant behavior. And, rather than being stigmatized as are many social deviants, these professional athletes are cheered, idolized, and highly paid (Carter & Carter 2007).

According to research done by Benedict and Yaeger (1998), one out of five NFL players has been charged with a serious criminal offense. In 1999, Blumstein and Benedict found that of the 509 NFL players they sampled, 109 had been arrested (21%). Many of these players had been arrested more than once (the 109 players had 264 arrests among them). To top it off, a number of players publish lucrative autobiographies (Green 1996; Sanders 1998; Taylor 2003; Romanowski 2005; Owens 2006) that have provided evidence of a wide array of deviant activities, both by their authors and by other NFL players. As a result, scholars, fans, sports organizations, and policy makers have become concerned about the behavior of professional athletes. Various organizations have voiced concern for the negative role models these players are providing for other athletes, particularly younger ones. The concern has far-reaching implications that are affecting more areas of American society than just football.

Moreover, the association of NFL players with an array of deviant behaviors such as illegal drugs, alcohol abuse, prostitution, and sexual misconduct, begs for a research-based explanation. The circumstances surrounding the arrests of high profile NFL players appears to be consistent with a growing trend toward various forms of deviance and illicit sexual behavior among players. These athletes' eccentric social environment, which produces numerous opportunities for players to deviate from traditional norms has been noted as a possible source of their deviance. According to Benedict (1997), "The temptation to indulge becomes acute for players who are routinely relieved of responsibility by their coaches and agents, while simultaneously being lauded and rewarded for doing what they desire most—to play ball" (63). Moreover, the sudden wealth and notoriety NFL players acquire further isolates them from society's established and traditional norms.

The study conducted for this book uses a blended methodological approach (Creswell 2005). Using Dexter's (1970) qualitative technique of elite and specialized interviewing in conjunction with Schatzman's and Strauss's (1973) naturalistic field method, access was gained into a select group of current and former NFL players. The qualitative findings in conjunction with the theoretical framework provided the conceptualization of a quantitative instrument. Through a snowball sample (Berg 2001), 104 NFL players were interviewed. A series of quantitative analyses was run to describe and assess levels of association within this sample.

Access to professional athletes, such as the 104 represented in this book, is extremely difficult to obtain. These athletes' private and professional lives are continually subject to criticism and embarrassment by peers, fans, the news media, and management during the normal course of their professional careers. They are subject daily to intense and critical scrutiny. For these reasons, as well as high levels of security, entrée typically cannot be gained without the help of informants (members of that social group) and the continuous establishment of reciprocity. In other words, not just any individual can walk into a team's facilities, practices, locker-rooms, and hotels, and gain access to players for in-depth interviews. One must have informants, and subsequently establish relationships with members of the study group. In essence, trustworthiness is a necessity; in this case I had to be viewed as one of the "boys."

The research findings discussed in this book are representative of these 104 players. I would further argue that this research provides interesting and possibly insightful associations among study variables. Moreover, the information and data contained in this book allow for the formation of additional questions which could affect policy decisions concerning both the lives of professional football players and related areas for future research.

Key Questions

For the research conducted for this book, I concentrated on three key questions for those NFL players who participated in this study. First, what are the factors that contribute to illegal behavior among NFL players who have been arrested, and to law-abiding conduct among those who have not? Although "deviance" does not necessarily mean "breaking the law," much of the questionable behaviors can be operationalized through this dichotomy. The second key question is whether levels of anomie can be measured among NFL players, and if so, what factors are associated with anomie. Third, and most important, are the players who reported themselves as law breakers the ones who exhibit anomic characteristics?

References

Bellah, Robert N. 1967. Religion in America. *Daedalus* 96: 1-21.

Benedict, Jeff. 1997. *Public heroes, private felons*. Boston: Northeastern University Press.

Benedict, Jeff, and Don Yaeger. 1998. *Pros and cons: The criminals who play in the NFL*. New York: Warner Books.

Berg, Bruce L. 2001. *Qualitative research methods for the social sciences*. Boston: Allyn and Bacon.

Blumstein, Alfred, and Jeff Benedict. 1999. Criminal violence of NFL players compared to the general population. *Chance* 12: 12-15.

Carter, Eric M. and Michael V. Carter. 2007. "A Social Psychological Analysis of Anomie Among National Football League Players." *International Review for the Sociology of Sport* 42: 243-270.

Coakley, Jay. 2007. *Sports and society: Issues and controversies*. Boston: McGraw Hill.

Creswell, John W. 2005. *Educational research: Planning, conducting, and evaluating quantitative and qualitative research*. Upper Saddle River, NJ: Pearson.

Dexter, Lewis A. 1970. *Elite and specialized interviewing*. Evanston: Northwestern University Press.

Durkheim, Emile. [1893] 1933. *The Division of Labor in Society*. Translated by George Simpson. New York: Free Press.

———. [1897] 1951. *Suicide*. Trans. John A. Spaulding and George Simpson. New York: Free Press.
———. [1912] 1965. *The elementary forms of religious life*. Trans. Joseph Ward Swain. New York: Free Press.
———. [1925] 1961. *Moral education*. Trans. Everett K. Wilson and Herman Schnurer. New York: Free Press.
Eitzen, Stanley D., ed. 2005. *Sport in contemporary society*. Boulder, CO: Paradigm Publishers.
Eitzen, Stanley D. and George H. Sage. 2009. *Sociology of North American sport*. Boulder, CO: Paradigm Publishers.
Green, Tim. 1996. *The dark side of the game: My life in the NFL*. New York: Warner Books.
Hirschi, Travis. 1969. *Causes of delinquency*. Berkeley: University of California Press.
Lowry, Tom. 2003. The NFL machine. *Business Week*, January 27.
MacCambridge, Michael. 2004. *America's game: The epic story of how pro football captured a nation*. New York: Random House.
Merton, Robert K. 1938. Social structure and anomie. *American Sociological Review* 3: 672-682.
Owens, Terrell, and Jason Rosenhaus. 2006. *T.O.* New York: Simon & Schuster.
Parsons, Talcott. 1937. *The structure of social action*. New York: McGraw Hill.
Romanowski, Bill, Adam Schefter, and Phil Towle. 2005. *Romo: My life on the edge*. New York: William Morrow.
Sage, George H. 1998. *Power and ideology in American sport: A critical perspective*. Champaign, IL: Human Kinetics.
Sanders, Deion, and Jim N. Black. 1998. *Power, money, & sex: How success almost ruined my life*. Nashville: Word Publishing.
Schatzman, Leonard, and Anselm L. Strauss. 1973. *Field research: Strategies for a natural sociology*. Englewood Cliffs, NJ: Prentice-Hall.
Starr, Mark, and Allison Samuels. 2000. A season of shame. *Newsweek*, May 29.
Taylor, Lawrence, and Steve Serby. 2003. *LT: Over the edge*. New York: HarperCollins.
Vaux, Alan. 1988. *Social support: Theory, research, and intervention*. New York: Praeger.

Chapter Two

It's Lonely (Anomie) at the Top: Theoretical Interpretations of Deviant Behavior

"I don't know what the hell happened to me . . . I'm so fucking miserable," one player told me. I asked him to elaborate. He responded, "I got caught, caught in the life, the money . . . my whole world changed so goddamn fast . . . I honestly can't explain it." This player was a star. Yet, two weeks prior to this conversation he had been arrested on weapons and drug charges. He was now staring at the end of his premature career. He had become a headline.

This story was not an outlier. It was in fact recited over and over by players I interviewed. Deviance like this among professional football players appeared to be a trend. So, I thought, there must be a theoretical explanation for the social deviance and illegal activities committed by so many professional football players.

In reviewing the multiple theories and perspectives concerning social deviance, two broad categories are considered. First, I examine perspectives based on culture and subculture (Cohen 1955) along with elements of learning theory (Sutherland 1947) and strain theory (Merton 1938). Initially, during formative stages of the qualitative field work, I thought that these perspectives, which concentrate on examining the subcultural and group behavior, would provide theoretical insight into the various forms of deviance exhibited by the NFL players studied. As discussed later, other perspectives emerged as more compatible with my data.

The second group of perspectives has their origin in classical Durkheimian theory and can be termed *theories of social disorganization*

(Park & Burgess 1921). These include classic anomie theory (Durkheim [1897] 1951), social control theory (Hirschi 1969), and social support theory (Vaux 1988). Although each of these theories and perspectives provides insights into various aspects of deviance and deviant behavior, I would argue that they have their origins in the classic research and writing of Emile Durkheim.

Today, much of our comprehension of social deviance rests in the formative works of Durkheim. Issues have been debated concerning appropriate levels of abstraction (macro versus micro) in regards to various aspects of Durkheimian theory (Parsons 1937; Marks 1974; Orru 1987). In essence, this debate points to whether or not Durkheim's theory is compatible with micro level data. This debate does have some utility. However, in an attempt to better understand Durkheim, it should not overshadow his ability to understand the impact of social change and social forces and move one's comprehension beyond mere individualistic (psychological) explanations of why deviance occurs within certain social groups. Most of Durkheim's research illustrates how social forces and structures influence the very nature of a given society. This contribution cannot be overstated; I would argue that it is perhaps one of the most important distinguishing findings in the history of social research and sociology in particular.

However, Durkheim ([1897] 1951) understood that these macro social forces left a definite impact on communities and individuals. This study applies Durkheim's theoretical insights about deviance to the study of contemporary professional athletes in the NFL. Just as Durkheim's empirical research examined subgroups within French society, this study examines a contemporary subgroup in American society. In Durkheim's analysis of suicide, he identified microsociological effects as a result of social change. In a similar fashion, this study attempts to identify the microsociological effects of social change on NFL players.

Additionally, a close look at Durkheim's ([1897] 1951) *Suicide* exposes a "multilevel theory of society that far surpasses its empirical foundations" (Thorlindsson & Bjarnason 1998: 94). Some scholars (Lukes 1972; Thorlindsson 1983) have argued that the reason Durkheim adopted a macrosociological approach to suicide was largely due to the aggregate nature of the data. But, "when Durkheim goes beyond the data to formulate a general theory of [anomie], he locates the major theoretical elements at the level of social relationships" (Thorlindsson & Bjarnason

1998: 94). Thus, one could argue that Durkheim, in his macro-level analysis, presupposes a social psychological perspective that he never "clearly" outlines.

Deviance Theories Based on Subcultural Learning Theories

Before examining Durkheim's theory and its derivatives, I should note that the initial assumption during the early stages of the field research was that culture/subculture played an important role in shaping the NFL players' deviant behaviors. I thought that perhaps NFL players learned deviance from other players in a deviant subculture. In other settings, scholars have theorized that culture presupposes a strong influence on individuals' behaviors and that "goals of action are set by culture" (Kornhauser 1978: 165). Moreover, I thought that differential association (Sutherland 1947) and aspects of strain theory (Merton 1938) could be valuable and compatible perspectives for this study.

Subcultural Theory

Proponents of subcultural theory typically assert that deviance is the result of a cultural system of values and beliefs that is more favorable to the use of deviant means than is the wider dominant culture (Wolfgang & Ferracuti 1967). Proponents assert that deviant subcultures emerge in response to unique issues that individuals of mainstream society typically do not face. Those immersed in a subculture of deviance engage in more pathological behaviors because the individuals and the group define deviance as *appropriate* in more situations than do those who ascribe to the dominant culture's beliefs, norms, and values view as inappropriate. Thus, people learn deviant behavior from deviant subcultures. If an individual is highly integrated into a deviant subculture, there is a higher probability that he/she will conform to the subcultural norms and values. In essence, the likelihood of "criminal [or deviant] behavior reaches its highest potential with the proliferation of subcultures, or subdivisions with beliefs and values at odds with the dominant culture" (Adler 2000: 280) (for further discussion of subcultural theory, see Cohen 1955; Cloward and Ohlin 1960; Wolfgang & Ferracuti 1967).

Differential Association Theory

Edwin Sutherland (1947) argued that deviance is learned and results from learning generally positive meanings of deviance through interaction with others, particularly intimates. This theory is based on the social environment, the individuals within that social environment, and the values those individuals acquire from others in the social environment. According to Sutherland, an individual becomes deviant due to an excess of definitions and meanings favorable to violation of the law or dominant social norms over definitions and meanings unfavorable to these violations. In essence, this theory focuses on "the connection between delinquent peers and the individual's delinquency" (Costello & Vowell 1999: 818) and the assumption that deviance is "explained largely in terms of positive relations with [deviant] others or others who present [deviant] patterns (model [deviance], present [deviant beliefs], and/or reinforce [deviance])" (Agnew 2000: 126) (for further discussion of differential association theory, see Sutherland 1947; Sutherland, Cressey, and Luckenbill 1992; Akers 1985).

Strain Theory

The basis of strain theory has roots in Durkheim's ([1897] 1951) theory of anomie. But a close examination reveals that the two are actually quite different (for further discussion of this debate, see Kornhauser 1978; Bernard 2000). The core idea behind strain theory is that individuals are *pressured* into deviance. There are typically two defining characteristics of strain theory. First, most "strain theorists argue that [deviance] results when individuals cannot get what they want through legitimate channels" (Agnew 2000: 113). Second, theorists argue that "frustrated wants *pressure or force* the person into [deviance]" (Agnew 2000: 114).

Robert Merton (1938) argued that this pressure comes from within a culture/subculture. In his classic paper, "Social Structure and Anomie," Merton argued that "our primary aim is to discover how *some social structures exert a definite pressure upon certain persons in the society to engage in nonconforming rather than conforming conduct*" (Merton 1968: 186). Moreover, according to Vold and Bernard (1986), "strain theories propose that there are certain socially generated pressures or forces that drive people to commit crimes [or deviance]" (185). In essence, subculturally prescribed goals and norms are key influences on individual behavior (for further discussion of strain theory, see Merton 1938; Cohen

1955; Cloward & Ohlin 1960; Agnew 1992, 2000; Messner & Rosenfeld 1994).

Incompatibility of Subcultural Learning Theories with Durkheim's Anomie

For purposes of this study, based on qualitative data and theoretical inconsistencies, I decided that the subcultural and learning theories were not appropriate frameworks from which to interpret deviance among NFL players. Once I decided Durkheim's ([1897] 1951) theory was more applicable, I determined that it would be difficult to merge subcultural and learning theories with the original sociological conception of anomie. For Durkheim, anomie is not "the result of strongly defined [sub]cultural goals" (Kornhauser 1978: 165). Anomie is not produced or created by culture or subculture. It is instead produced by the weakness or *absence* of culture. For Durkheim, deviance does not result from strain but from "the absence of strong social bonds or effective cultural regulation" (Kornhauser 1978: 165). According to Kornhauser (1978),

> Anomie . . . does not refer to a culture characterized by strong goals and weak means; it refers to a weak culture that fails to define the goals of human endeavor. Culture does not enjoin man to have limitless aspirations. Man's limitless aspirations are given in the human condition. We are all strained. Culture *limits* aspirations. A culture characterized by anomie no longer supplies the limits to aspiration. (165-166)

If culture fails to demarcate the goals of healthy economic endeavor, the result is unlimited yearning and greed. When passions are given free rein, the definition is typically a state of strain, as these unleashed passions are not capable of being fulfilled. Few individuals know when they have earned enough money or gained enough status and power. The failure of a culture "to relate these values to other values, in an appropriate *hierarchy* of value, is the root of anomie" (Kornhauser 1978: 166). Thus, culture is not the cause of strain, as Merton would have us believe.

When a culture is weak or nonexistent, the "strain that inheres in the human condition becomes manifest" (Kornhauser 1978: 166). For if success goals, whether they be deviant or mainstream, were effectively defined, they would not cause strain or anomie. However, "when anomie unleashes strain, it brings men to an anguished confrontation with meaninglessness. Since desire that has no [clear and achievable] goal can ever be satisfied, the endless striving to achieve gratifications that recede in their consummation is meaningless" (Kornhauser 1978: 166). Thus, an appropriate conceptualization of anomie is meaninglessness. One who lacks meaning is despondent, which is a reflection of the emptiness created by action that has no clear or achievable goal. And, in many cases, the end result of despair or anomie is deviance.

Deviance Theories Based on Social Disorganization

After deciding that a subcultural approach would not be fruitful, I examined several other perspectives. Aspects of social control theory (Hirschi 1969) and social support theory (Vaux 1988), which are Durkheimian in nature, are consistent with Durkheim's ([1897] 1951) conception of anomie and helped make sense of the qualitative data. These perspectives incorporate factors (social support/ties) I thought were important for addressing the deviant behavior of the NFL players. In essence, the inductive nature of the research helped me identify and specify the appropriate theory.

Social Control Theory

Social control theorists assert that deviance results from the absence or breakdown of positive relationships with other conventional individuals and institutions. Individuals who do not have *ties* to other conventional individuals or institutions are not forced or pressured into deviance, as strain theory argues, but are *free* to deviate. Thus, they often engage in deviance "as they seek to satisfy universal human needs [and wants] in the most expedient manner" (Agnew 2000: 118).

Travis Hirschi ([1969] 2005) played a key role in the development of this theory in his classic work *Causes of Delinquency*. He credits "important elements of the perspective to the likes of . . . Durkheim" (*xv*). Hirschi maintains that *conformity* must be explained rather than crime or deviance. Hirschi ([1969] 2005) refers to the forces controlling or influencing deviant behavior as the *social bond* and notes that this perspective "starts from the straightforward assumption that deviant behavior occurs when the bond of the individual to society is weak or broken" (*xvii*).

Social control theory "assumes the existence of a common value system within the society" (Hirschi 1969: 23) and argues "that if social control institutions, that is, the various mechanisms by which behavior is organized and channeled into the requirements of the social order, remain intact, they can serve to maintain a stable social order despite social change" (Adler 2000: 276). When social control is unsuccessful (social institutions breakdown or there is a weak culture/subculture) its proponents expect that rates of deviance or unlawful behavior will rise.

For Durkheim ([1897] 1951) who is largely regarded as a social control theorist (Kornhauser 1978), rapid social or economic change creates the deregulation and malintegration of the social group and is the basis of disorder and pathology in society. In a stable and regulated culture/subculture, individuals are immersed in a "secure environment with familial, religious, economic, and communal social controls firmly intact" (Adler 2000: 278). But when rapid social or economic change occurs, the common rules and norms of the group are thrown into disarray. Thus, "individual desires are no longer regulated by a moral force provided by the 'collective conscience'" (Adler 2000: 278). For Durkheim ([1897] 1951), human wants and desires are boundless, an "insatiable and bottomless abyss" (247). In essence, it is social rules and norms that keep human aspiration in check. These regulations are internalized "into the individual conscience and thus make it possible for people to feel fulfilled" (Adler 2000: 278).

Social Support Theory

A close relative of social control theory (Vaux 1988), social support theory is concerned with the importance of social ties. Durkheim ([1897] 1951), in his classic study of suicide, highlighted the significance of weakened social ties to family, community, and religion. He argued that in times of rapid social or economic change, if social ties or bonds were weak or diminishing, a state of anomie could ensue. This resulting state of anomie, he argued, led to deviant forms of behavior such as suicide and found that suicide was most common among groups with weak social ties.

Later, the "Chicago School" of sociology reiterated the view that disrupted or weak social ties led to social-psychological and social problems. This Durkheimian-based work which linked social disintegration to social-psychological disorders set the stage for the contemporary work on social support and "the idea that morale and well-being are sustained through primary group ties, the absence of which may result in a loss of identity, confusion regarding norms, and despair, echoes the contemporary discussions of social support" (Vaux 1988: 2).

John Cassel (1974), Gerald Caplan (1974), and Sidney Cobb (1976), who laid the groundwork for contemporary social support theory, argued that social support works to buffer the individual from the adverse effects of stress and social change. Social support provided by primary social ties/groups can serve "an important protective function, 'buffering' or 'cushioning' the individual from the . . . psychological consequences of stressful experiences" (Vaux 1988: 6). The social ties important to social support range from social integration to intimate relationships to social networks (for further discussion, see Vaux 1988).

In relation to social support and anomie, "the existing evidence suggests that social support has direct and buffering effects on [deviance]" (Cullen & Wright 1997: 194). Recent research (Wright 1996; Wright, Cullen & Wooldredge 1995) has shown that family structural variables such as parental or spousal supports, poverty, and "broken homes" have an influence on deviance. Thus, a person's social ties provided by the relationships found within the family and community, religion, marriage, and education are thought to influence (or buffer) the likelihood of anomie and deviance.

Nan Lin (1986) describes social support as "the perceived or actual instrumental and/or expressive provisions supplied by the community, social networks, and confiding partners" (18). Thus, according to Cullen and Wright (1997), anomie does not "lead ineluctably to ill-health, for effects might be diminished if a person were to be enmeshed in social relationships that provide support" (193). In essence, these support factors provide social ties that appear to create some sense of boundaries and limits for behavior. On the other hand, the lack of social ties and bonds supplied by a support system appears to provide the opposite: weakened structures, few boundaries, and few limits; hence anomic conditions.

Anomie Theory

Anomie can be described as a state of *deregulation* and *malintegration* (Durkheim [1897] 1951), and at the personal or individual level, a state of meaninglessness or unhappiness (Durkheim [1897] 1951; Srole 1956;

Kornhauser 1978). This state is typically brought about by sudden economic change. For Durkheim, anomie was a "corrupted and pathological condition" (Orru 1987: 4) of a normal social system, a social institution/group, or an individual. Anomie is thus "both a social condition and a psychic state, a general aimlessness accompanied by feelings of emptiness" (Powell 1970: 8). In essence, an individual becomes lost in a void of meaninglessness, confused by a rapidly changing milieu. According to Parsons ([1937] 1968), "*Anomie* is precisely this state of disorganization where the hold of norms over individual conduct has broken down" (377).

Anomie: The Construct

Despite the fact that the construct of anomie is quite recent, its roots go back more than twenty-five centuries. Anomie (*anomia*) is Greek in origin and, in essence, means absence of law (Orru 1987). The meaning of anomie varies greatly throughout the literature and reflects the specific concerns of different time periods and cultures.

For example, anomie means "ruthlessness and *hybris* in Euripides, anarchy and intemperance in Plato, sin and wickedness in the Old Testament, unrighteousness or unwritten law in Paul's letters, irregularity or formal transgression in Bishop Bramhall's treatises, a positive characteristic of modern morality in Jean Marie Gayau's works," (Orru 1987: 2) and a human state of insatiability and the absence of social restraints on human aspirations in Durkheim ([1893] 1933, [1897] 1951). For more contemporary thinkers, it indicates a conflict of belief-systems in a society or "separation anxiety" (de Grazia 1948: 47-76), "social and emotional void" (Wirth 1951: xxv), the imbalance between cultural goals and institutional means at either the social or individual level or "normlessness" (Merton 1938), "the nightmare *par excellence*, in which the individual is submerged in a world of disorder, senselessness and madness" (Berger 1967: 22), a social-psychological condition of malintegration and self-to-other alienation (Srole 1956), or even "meaninglessness" and unhappiness (Powell 1970: 8). For an excellent historical analysis of the meanings of anomie, see Marco Orru's *Anomie: History and Meanings* (1987).

For this study, however, the core conceptualization of anomie that will be applied is Durkheimian in nature. More specifically it is a multidimensional construct that encompasses: (a) rapid life change, (b) confusion and anxiety, (c) disconnectedness, (d) greed and gratification, (e) unhappiness and discontent, and (f) meaninglessness and lack of purpose. In short, it is a series of social psychological attributes, a state of individual or group normlessness, that is typically brought about by sudden prosperity. See Figure 1.

Figure 1: Conceptual Model for Anomie

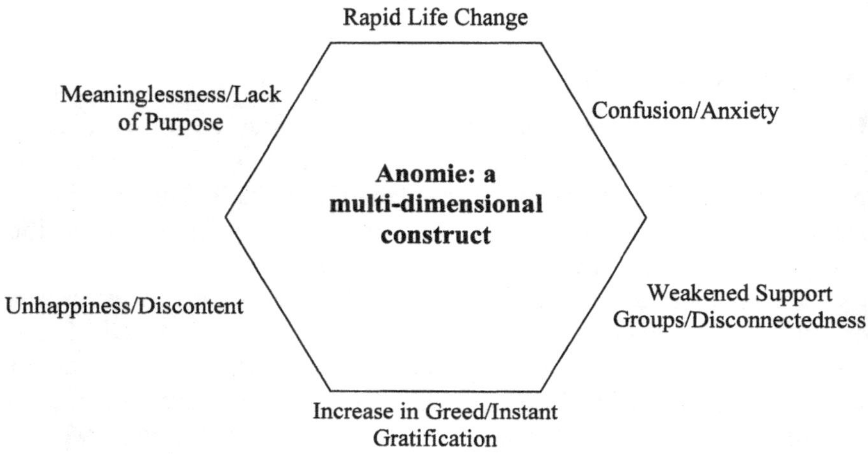

A hexagonal diagram with "Anomie: a multi-dimensional construct" in the center, surrounded by six labels: Rapid Life Change (top), Confusion/Anxiety (upper right), Weakened Support Groups/Disconnectedness (lower right), Increase in Greed/Instant Gratification (bottom), Unhappiness/Discontent (lower left), Meaninglessness/Lack of Purpose (upper left).

Durkheim's Conception of Anomie

Durkheim ([1893] 1933) first used the term anomie in *The Division of Labor in Society*. In this work, he was concerned with the problem of how a society with a high degree of social differentiation was able to maintain social cohesion (Clinard 1964). The concept of a "division of labor" in society contributed greatly to our understanding of social differentiation. He argued that an "increasingly complex division of labor would make social relationships so unstable that society could only be held together by some external mechanism" or form of social control such as the state or other social structure (Clinard 1964: 3).

In assessing this problem, Durkheim ([1893] 1933) distinguished between two types of unity in a society: the *mechanical solidarity* of simpler societies and the *organic solidarity* of contemporary, complex,

Western societies (Clinard 1964). Organic solidarity was a result of the nature of people's relationships in a society having a wide-ranging division of labor, centered on "specialization of function and resulting differences among individuals" (Clinard 1964: 4). It was important, however, that extensive contacts between diverse groups in a society emerge in order to attain a degree of organic solidarity. One would associate this type of society with the industrialization and increasing urbanization of the late nineteenth and early twentieth centuries. Durkheim argued that, "in undifferentiated societies characterized by mechanical solidarity, a single *collective conscience*" based on likeness and common interests directs most individuals (Clinard 1964: 4). Such societies were rural and agricultural in nature. Durkheim believed that in the more differentiated societies where the division of labor and organic solidarity abound, the collective conscience weakens and individual differences are supported.

Durkheim ([1893] 1933) also identified three *abnormal* forms of the division of labor. In connection with these, he introduced the concept of anomie (Clinard 1964). One of these forms was the forced division of labor, in which the allocation of occupations does not follow the allocation of talent or skills. In a second type of situation, the division of labor does not generate solidarity because the functional activity of each worker is inadequate; the worker does not acquire a sense of participation in a common endeavor. The third and predominant abnormal condition, however, he characterized as *anomic* (Clinard 1964). This indicated a lack of integration or adjustment of functions rising out of industrial crises. Anomie or anomic conditions arise "because the division of labor fails to produce sufficiently effective contacts between its members and adequate regulation of social relationships" (Clinard 1964: 4). In other words, as worker specialization increased and economic changes continued, people felt "without regulation;" life itself has changed and appeared to be in constant flux.

Anomie played a reasonably small part in Durkheim's theory of the division of labor. He used it simply to describe one of the "abnormal forms that resulted in imperfect organic solidarity" (Clinard 1964: 4). It was in his classic study of suicide that anomie took on its great theoretical importance. This is where Durkheim ([1897] 1951) formulated his idea that deviant behaviors, such as suicide, were related to anomie and where he made his case for the explanatory role of anomie. For Durkheim, the great variations in the rate of suicide were associated with the business cycle. But, while the likelihood of suicide during an economic depression might appear easy to explain, the increase of suicide during periods of unusual or sudden prosperity was a much more difficult task. Durkheim said that suicide could occur in *both* periods because "people [were] suddenly being thrown out of adjustment with their typical ways of life, sudden economic prosperity being as disastrous as sudden loss" (Clinard 1964: 5). In both cases, there is a sense of uncertainty and chaos, and people become disoriented. Under these conditions, most people no longer felt that they were making progress with reference to what they wanted and desired. This important insight, that the *rate* of social change, and not its direction, was responsible for increases in anomie, set the tone for subsequent research on social change and the effects of anomie.

Following Durkheim, Parsons (1937) pointed out that sudden prosperity, with a subsequent increase in deviance, resulted in a situation where "a sense of security, of progress toward ends depends not only on adequate command over means, but on a clear definition of the ends themselves" (335). When people "achieve sudden prosperity, which they had thought impossible to achieve, they tend no longer to believe in the impossibility of anything" (Clinard 1964: 5). Thus, the breakdown or failure of controls over an individual's desires in a society and of socially accepted norms and standards, especially when change is sudden, gives rise to conditions that may lead to deviant acts such as suicide. It was this type of suicide that Durkheim called "*anomic suicide*," proposing that the condition was one of anomie. His research showed that there was a high rate of such suicides among those who were affluent. Sudden upward changes in one's standard of living tends to put norms in flux. Situations as such "become functional equivalents of depressions, in which the regulatory functions of the collective order break down" (Clinard 1964: 5).

For Durkheim ([1897] 1951), a deviant act such as suicide "was not an individual phenomenon but was related to certain characteristics of the social organization" (Clinard 1964: 6). These characteristics "were the degree of control or regulation in a society, the amount of group unity, and the strength of ties binding people together" (Clinard 1964: 6). A unified and well-regulated society or culture can diminish anomic currents. Such *social facts* are typically to be explained with reference to society or its structures and not necessarily with reference to the individual (Clinard 1964). However, "when the theory of anomie is elaborated in the middle of *Suicide*, it is . . . in most respects a microsociological theory" (Marks 1974:331). For Durkheim ([1897] 1951), disturbed and interrupted group life produces unregulated individuals with "insatiable appetites" and "fevered imaginations" (254).

Deviant acts such as suicides arising from a state of anomie were, therefore, products of the failure of social restraints on what might be called "overweening ambitions" (Clinard 1964: 7). As Durkheim ([1897] 1951) wrote, "human activity naturally aspires beyond assignable limits and sets itself unattainable goals" (247-248). This idea reflected the view that individuals are "filled with certain innate desires which needed to be fulfilled and that society either restrained or encouraged them" (Clinard 1964: 7). An individual's natural "needs must be regulated by the moral needs defined and regulated by the collective order" (Clinard 1964: 7).

What Durkheim referred to as anomie can otherwise be termed a state of *deregulation*, or on the microsociological level, meaninglessness (Srole 1956). Some have even interpreted it (from the original French) as *dereglement* or *derangement* (Mestrovic & Brown 1985) with which there are connotations of immorality, madness, and sin. This condition arises when a disturbance of the collective order allows people's aspirations to rise past all prospect of fulfillment (Clinard 1964). People aspire to goals that they cannot attain or find difficult to reach. Appearing more to describe and explain the present than the society and cultures of his day, Durkheim spelled out the characteristics, principally economic, of a society or culture that produces "unlimited aspirations" and hence anomic behaviors (Clinard 1964: 7). As Durkhiem ([1897] 1951) described it,

> Actually religion has lost most of its power. And government, instead of regulating economic life, has become its tool and servant. . . . On both sides nations are declared to have the single or chief purpose of achieving . . . prosperity; such is the implication of the dogma of economic materialism, the basis of both apparently opposed systems. And as these theories merely express the state of opinion, industry instead of being still regarded as a means to an end transcending itself, has become the supreme end of individuals and societies alike. Thereupon the appetites thus excited have become freed of any limiting authority. . . . Such is the source of the excitement predominating in this part of society, and which has thence extended to other parts. There, the state of crisis and anomy is constant and, so to speak, normal. From top to bottom of the ladder, greed is aroused without knowing where to find an ultimate foothold. Nothing can calm it, since its goal is far beyond all it can attain. Reality seems valueless by comparison

with the dreams of fevered imaginations; reality is therefore abandoned, but so too is possibility abandoned when it in turn becomes reality. A thirst arises for novelties: Unfamiliar pleasures, nameless sensations, all of which lose their savor once known. Henceforth, one has no strength to endure the least reverse. The whole fever subsides and the sterility of all the tumult is apparent, and it is seen that all these new sensations in their infinite quantity cannot form a solid foundation of happiness to support one during days of trial. The wise man, knowing how to enjoy achieved results without having constantly to replace them with others, finds in them an attachment to life in the hour of difficulty. But the man who has always pinned all his hopes on the future and lived with his eyes fixed upon it, has nothing in the past as a comfort against the present afflictions, for the past was nothing to him but a series of hastily experienced stages. What blinded him to himself was his expectation always to find, further on, the happiness he had so far missed. Now he is stopped in his tracks; from now on nothing remains behind or ahead of him to fix his gaze upon. Weariness alone, moreover, is enough to bring disillusionment, for he cannot in the end escape the futility of an endless pursuit. . . . We may even wonder if this moral state is not principally what makes economic catastrophes of our day so fertile in suicides. (255-256)

Durkheim also pointed out the importance of social ties/bonds, and noted that stable societies or cultures are the ones in which definite and reasonable goals help the individual respect normative bounds. Economic goals are, in many cases, more clearly characterized and typically fall within the aspirations of the individual (Clinard 1964).

This relative limitation and the moderation it involves, make men contented with their lot while stimulating them moderately to improve it; and this average contentment causes the feeling of calm, active happiness, the pleasure in existing and living which characterizes health for societies as well as for individuals. Each person is then at least, generally speaking, in harmony with his condition, and desires only what he may legitimately hope for as the normal reward for his activity. Besides, this does not condemn man to a sort of immobility. . . . For, loving what he has and not fixing his desire solely on what he lacks, his wishes and hopes may fail of what he has happened to aspire to, without his being wholly destitute. He has the essentials. The equilibrium of his happiness is secure because it is defined, and a few mishaps cannot disconcert him. (Durkheim [1897] 1951: 250)

Forms of Anomie

Durkheim ([1893] 1933; [1897] 1951) discussed two forms of anomie—*chronic* and *acute*. Both were a result of an imbalance between means and needs (states of disequilibrium), where means were inadequate to fulfill needs. But it is important to differentiate between these two types of anomie.

Chronic Anomie

Durkheim's analysis of chronic anomie focuses not on sudden social or economic change, but rather on the consequences of the gradual decrease of social regulation. The premise of chronic anomie, "is conceived as a permanent disease of industrial societies" (Besnard 1988: 92). According to Durkheim ([1897] 1951), industry has come to be viewed as an end in itself since the restraint over economic (industrial) relations that was typically exercised by religion, civil authority, and occupational groups has eroded over time (Thompson 1982). Consequently, in the industrial context, the individual is freed from social restraint, while integrative mechanisms are weakened. Thus, chronic anomie "expresses the fact that the social world is change in itself and is a permanent lack of stable references" (Besnard 1988: 92).

The degree of restraint, in the midst of unsteady references and social ties, that the individual can endure is proportional to the amount that the individual experiences. Therefore, the weakening of restraint and integration makes remaining restraint appear intolerable. This is even more true for the fortunate and affluent than it is for the poor. Durkheim ([1897] 1951) noted that in modern societies and cultures, the deregulated state is elevated to a virtue: "The longing for infinity is daily represented as a mark of moral distinction, whereas it can only appear within unregulated consciences which elevate to a rule the lack of rule from which they suffer" (257). In essence, chronic anomie is not a product of temporary or the sudden absence of rules and norms. It results from "the presence, in modern culture, of the doctrine of constant progress, the longing for infinity, the necessity for a person to advance constantly toward an indefinite goal" (Besnard 1988: 92).

Chronic Anomic Currents in Professional Football

Chronic anomic conditions arise when industry or occupational groups such as the NFL (within modern culture) are in a state of constant social change and there is a disappearance of many regulatory norms. According to Durkheim ([1897] 1951), "the sphere of trade and industry . . . is actually in a chronic state" (255). This is the state of modern professional sport in America, which during the last 50 years has undergone substantial change (Eitzen & Sage 2009).

The industry of professional football has been one of the most successful growth industries in recent decades (Lowry 2003; MacCambridge 2004). To understand the roots of change in the NFL, we must turn back to 1960 when the newly-appointed commissioner Pete Rozelle persuaded the government to pass the Sports Broadcasting Act. This allowed sports leagues to sell broadcast rights as a package and ultimately allowed them to negotiate more favorable contracts. Shortly thereafter, the NFL reached its first deal with CBS. CBS agreed to pay the NFL $4.6 million, which would be split among the teams. With this accomplishment, Rozelle was credited "with transforming modern sports by marrying games with TV" (Lowry 2003: 91). This transformation arguably brought about the emergence of chronic anomic conditions within the industry because "government, instead of regulating economic life, [had] become its tool and servant" (Durkheim [1897] 1951: 255).

Even the professional football visionaries could not have imagined the television riches brought by fans' hunger for NFL games. The NFL's current network and satellite television contracts with ESPN, NBC, FOX, CBS, and DirectTV will bring the league $3.75 billion a year through 2011 (Yost 2006). Today, relying largely on television revenue, the NFL is a $1 billion a year business with each franchise worth over $550 million (Eitzen & Sage 2009).

The economic change associated with the emergence of the Sports Broadcasting Act, and then through free agency in the 1990s, has set up the NFL to have one of the most favorable player deals in professional sports. On average, athletes receive $1.4 million in salary (USA Today 2007), a figure that continues to rise (which does not include large signing bonuses). For example, Philadelphia Eagles quarterback Donovan McNabb made $21.7 million in 2003, the majority of which came from his signing bonus. With these chronic changes in the industry of the NFL, come the "pluses and minuses associated with players who are larger than life" (Lowry 2003: 87). As Durkheim ([1897] 1951) said, "industry, instead of being still regarded as a means to an end transcending itself, has become the supreme end of individuals. . . . Thereupon the appetites thus excited have become freed of any limiting authority" (255).

Acute Anomie

For Durkheim ([1897] 1951), the anomie of affluence is a result of rapid and extreme changes in wealth. This type of anomie is what Durkheim termed acute anomie. Acute anomie is central to this study and helps explain why economic crises (sudden fortune) help increase social deviance.

According to Pope (1976), "central to the explanation [of acute anomie] is the means-needs balance" (25). The key consideration is whether an individual's means are adequate for the fulfillment of his or her needs. Where means are proportional to needs, Durkheim ([1897] 1951) noted, they exist in a state of equilibrium. And, on the other hand, where the means are inadequate to fulfill the needs, they exist in a state of disequilibrium. These needs are not given by an individual's biological, psychological, or individual nature, but are social products that differ from one social context to the next (Thompson 1982). In many cases, "particular goals, desires, passions, or appetites for comfort, well-being, and luxury may become translated into needs" (Pope 1976: 25). Durkheim used needs in a general sense to include all of these things. Moreover, he spoke of needs, ends, and goals, or the passions, appetites, and desires that can turn a want into a need.

Durkheim ([1897] 1951) believed that human wants are boundless and insatiable, and, "unless restrained they represent a constant threat to individual happiness" (Pope 1976: 25). Far from serving to fulfill and satisfy the individual, the satisfaction of needs only serves to stimulate additional needs. Thus, the essential element for equilibrium between means and needs is some external force or social control mechanism that limits individual desires. Because most people cannot do this themselves, an external restraint is necessary. For Durkheim ([1897] 1951), the needs in question are moral in nature. Because structures are the only superior moral power whose authority and regulation individuals accept, only societies, cultures, or other social structures can provide the required restraint and control. Restrained by this societal pressure, each individual "in his sphere" accepts the "limit set to his ambitions and aspires to nothing beyond" (Durkheim [1897] 1951: 250).

For Durkheim ([1897] 1951), this is the way equilibrium is sustained under normal conditions. But, during periods of crisis characterized by abrupt changes, society and its institutions become unable to exercise their usual regulatory and moral authority. In the case of economic depression, people are cast into a new and lower state. This forces them to scale down their goals. And, "although the old rules are no longer applicable to an individual's new situation, new ones appropriate to that situation cannot be instantly established" (Pope 1976: 26). As a result, individuals find it difficult to adjust to their new situation, and their subsequent suffering "detaches them from a reduced existence even before they have made trial of it" (Durkheim [1897] 1951: 252). For similar reasons, sudden wealth and prosperity also creates a disjunction between means and needs. This disjunction is particularly severe because "the richer prize offered" stimulates them, making them even less agreeable to restraint (Durkheim [1897] 1951: 253).

Durkheim ([1897] 1951) observed that there were remarkably low rates of deviant behavior, such as suicide, among the poor. He stated that, "actual possessions are partly the criterion of those aspired to," so that the more an individual has, the more that individual wants (254). Pope (1976) elaborated, "having little, the poor aspire to little; thus their means tend to be adequate for their needs" (26). By contrast, wealth "by the power it bestows, deceives us into believing that we depend on ourselves only," thereby encouraging opposition to collective social rules and regulation and suggesting the possibility of unlimited success against the opposition "we encounter from objects" (Durkheim [1897] 1951: 254). Ironically, by virtue of having more, the affluent experience a greater means-needs imbalance than do the poor.

In essence, Durkheim ([1897] 1951) related sudden change to society's ability to moderate aspirations. During times of abrupt change, society's regulatory impact is weakened. Individuals find themselves in new and different situations to which the old rules do not seem to apply. As a result, they are freed from social restraint, their needs increasingly outstrip their means, and the consequent disequilibrium creates more unhappiness and a state of meaninglessness, which manifests itself in deviant behavior.

Acute Anomic Currents in Professional Football

The media's marketing of sports (NFL) celebrities as cult figures and their subsequent commodification has promoted the huge salaries and over-hyped celebrity status of professional athletes. These multi-million dollar salaries and the status, power, and influence that comes with them changes athletes' lives instantly. Moreover, sports stars today set the benchmark for aspiration and material wealth in contemporary popular culture (Whannel 2002). In essence, the chronic anomic currents in the industry have contributed to the acute anomic crises for individual NFL players. Moreover, it appears that chronic and acute change in the industry, multi-million dollar salaries and signing bonuses, have a dramatic impact on player behavior and lifestyles. In other words, acute changes in wealth among the individual NFL players may be associated with *personal anomie* and deviance.

Furthermore, the sudden life change that accompanies the instant wealth and power of professional football players can be conceptualized as the basis of acute anomie. For Durkheim ([1897] 1951), acute anomie is conceived as a "disease of the infinite" (Besnard 1988: 93), a "sickness" (Cohen 1972: 329). He pointed out the implications of abrupt changes and accentuated how anomie could result from improvements in economic and material conditions. He cautioned, for example, "of the moral danger involved in every growth of prosperity . . . wealth . . . suggests the possibility of unlimited success" (Durkheim ([1897] 1951: 254). Additionally, it appears in many cases that the wealth acquired by NFL players gives them "a sense of power and supremacy that deceives them into believing that they are answerable only to themselves" (Abrahamson 1980: 50).

Interpreting Durkheim's ([1897] 1951) prescient descriptions of "unfamiliar pleasures" and "nameless sensations," that describe the lifestyle of many professional football players, Harry Cohen (1972) states,

> In the anomic drive for power, prestige, money and the materialistic things that these can buy . . . there is no end, no ultimate satisfaction. . . . There is never enough because the accumulation of wealth is external, and the rewards are not internal in terms of deeper personal and personality gratification and such. In addition, wealth is always relative; there is always more to be had . . . he sees only more ahead, and keeps running, never reaching his goal. Anomic people do not know why they strive so, why they still miss something when they are richer and richer, their houses bigger and their earnings better . . . life remains truly meaningless. (330-331)

The Social Psychological Level of Anomie

Durkheim ([1897] 1951) typically discussed anomie as a macro-sociological problem. As he used the concept, anomie referred to the traits of a social institution/group or the social structure, and not necessarily to the traits of individuals. Although Durkheim's conception of anomie is conceived as a societal level phenomenon, his incredible insight into human behavior can be used to assess social psychological evaluations (different levels of abstraction) as well. Passas (2000) maintains that "the object of analysis may be a given society . . . as it may be a particular section of society . . . or [a] social institution" (106). In essence, an individual's social psychological or personal anomie is typically a manifestation of an anomic social group or institution. As Parsons ([1937] 1968) argued, "the social and psychopathological explanations of [deviance] are not antithetical but complementary" (326).

Many scholars realized that anomie was a powerful social phenomenon that was prevalent in certain social situations. With Durkheim's, seemingly only macro-level, conception locked in the sociological "iron cage" and with the pressing need to look at the social psychological aspects of anomie, the concept of *anomia* was developed (MacIver 1950; Riesman, Glazor, & Denney 1956; Srole 1956). Robert MacIver (1950) conceptualized anomia as "a state of mind in which the individual's sense of social cohesion—the mainspring of his morale—is broken or fatally weakened" (85), while David Riesman (1956) described the anomic individual as "maladjusted." As individuals feel more and more detached, "they lose their motivation to behave morally in the context of that [social] system" (Cohen 2000:189).

Leo Srole (1956) developed a social psychological measure of anomia that "refers to the degree of felt social connectedness of actors" (Lovell-Troy 1983:303). Orru (1987) argues that,

> the background assumption of Srole's scale is that the desirable condition of social systems is characterized at the macrosocial (molar) level by the 'integratedness' of different social systems or subsystems, and at the microsocial (molecular) level by the functional integration of individuals in relation to the social normative situation. Anomia expresses the malintegration or dysfunctional relation of individuals to their social worlds. (126)

In other words, the individual with anomic characteristics will seem to be disconnected from: (a) the larger political norms of society; (b) the larger cultural norms of society; (c) the larger economic norms of society; (d) "internalized social norms and values"; and (e) the main socialization group (Srole 1956: 711). Moreover, many scholars (MacIver 1950; McClosky & Shaar 1965; Srole 1956) have said that anomia has two key aspects: (a) disconnectedness from and malintegration into the normative structures of society, and (b) deregulation or disrupted/inadequate socialization. Both of these key aspects are important components in this analysis of the negative consequences of sudden change in the lives of professional football players.

At the individual level, disruptions such as sudden wealth and power can weaken their sense of belonging, leading to anormative behaviors of many NFL players. This, in turn, produces anomia at the individual or social psychological level. Anomia occurs because of "deficiencies at the level of specific groups" (Marks 1974:334). For this study, these deficiencies occur at the institutional level and at the individual level of NFL players. Regardless of the level of measurement and the different causes of anomie/anomia, "the concept itself refers to the same idea/ phenomenon: a weakening of the guiding power of social norms, a loosened social control" (Passas 2000:106-107).

Summary of Theoretical Understandings

In summary, social disorganization theory suggests that identifiable characteristics should be found that contribute to two distinct groups within the NFL: players who live within the bounds of normative behavior and players who display deviant characteristics. Subcultural and learning theories were initially thought to be useful in identifying some of these characteristics. On the other hand, their differences with Durkheimian literature and qualitative data make them less compatible.

However, some elements of subcultural and learning theories could be used at several points during this study. One could make the case that a certain group is bounded via a subculture. Much in the same vein, it could be cited that learning takes place through various circumstances and thus becomes a useful paradigm. Nonetheless, there appeared to be much more evidence that NFL players were part of a *weak* culture rather than a subculture. If players were indeed enmeshed in a subculture then they would likely have some level of social support, as even deviant subcultures provide social bonds. And, if deviant subcultures provide social ties and support, it could be argued that players would be integrated and would likely be less anomic. However, qualitative data suggested that these players' culture was weak, with few ties and support mechanisms. This appeared to be a key factor in why players exhibited anomic characteristics and elements of deviance. In essence, this indicated that many of the players typically did not learn deviance via their subculture.

Thus, Durkheim's theory of anomie, and related themes of social control and social support, provides the theoretical framework for this study of deviant behaviors in the NFL. In addressing possible factors associated with those NFL players who are law breakers (or engage in deviant behaviors), Durkheim's theory suggests that rapid change in wealth could be a plausible explanation. According to Powell (1970), "crime [or deviance] flourishes under conditions . . . of anomie" (107). Moreover, for those who appear to be anomic, weak social ties (social control and social support factors) may perpetuate this condition. Thus, is deviance in the NFL a product of anomie?

References

Adler, Freda. 2000. Synnomie to anomie: A macrosociological formulation. In *The Legacy of Anomie Theory*, ed. Freda Adler and William S. Laufer, 271-283. New Brunswick, NJ: Transaction Publishers.

Agnew, Robert. 1992. Foundation for a general strain theory. *Criminology* 30: 40-87.

———. 2000. The contribution of social-psychological strain theory to the explanation of crime and delinquency. In *The Legacy of Anomie Theory*, ed. Freda Adler and William S. Laufer, 113-137. New Brunswick, NJ: Transaction Publishers.

Akers, Ronald L. 1985. *Deviant Behavior: A Social Learning Approach*. Belmont, CA: Wadsworth.

Berger, Peter L. 1967. *The Sacred Canopy*. New York: Doubleday.

Bernard, Thomas J. 2000. Merton versus Hirschi: Who is faithful to Durkheim's heritage? In *The Legacy of Anomie Theory*, ed. Freda Adler and William S. Laufer, 81-90. New Brunswick, NJ: Transaction Publishers.

Besnard, Philippe. 1988. The true nature of anomie. *Sociological Theory* 6: 91-95.
Caplan, Gerald. 1974. *Support systems and community mental health: Lectures on concept development.* New York: Behavioral Publications.
Cassel, John. 1974. Psychosocial processes and "stress": Theoretical formulations. *International Journal of Health Services* 4: 471-482.
Clinard, Marshall B., ed. 1964. *Anomie and deviant behavior.* New York: Free Press.
Cloward, Richard, and Lloyd Ohlin. 1960. *Delinquency and opportunity.* New York: Free Press.
Cobb, Sidney. 1976. Social support as a moderator of life stress. *Psychosomatic Medicine* 38: 300-314.
Cohen, Albert K. 1955. *Delinquent boys.* New York: Free Press.
Cohen, Deborah V. 2000. Ethics and crime in business firms: Organizational culture and the impact of anomie.183-206 In *The legacy of anomie theory*, ed. Freda Adler and William S. Laufer, 183-206. New Brunswick, NJ: Transaction Publishers.
Cohen, Harry. 1972. The anomia of success and the anomia of failure: A study of similarities in opposites. *The British Journal of Sociology* 23: 329-343.
Costello, Barbara J., and Paul R. Vowell. 1999. Testing control theory and differential association: A reanalysis of the Richmond youth project data. *Criminology* 37: 815-843.
Cullen, Francis T., and John Paul Wright. 1997. Liberating the anomie-strain paradigm: Implications from social-support theory. In *The future of anomie theory*, eds. Nikos Passas and Robert Agnew, 187-206. Boston: Northeastern University Press.
de Grazia, Sebastian. 1948. *The political community: A study of anomie.* Chicago: University of Chicago Press.
Durkheim, Emile. [1893] 1933. *The Division of Labor in Society.* Translated by George Simpson. New York: Free Press.
———. [1897] 1951. *Suicide.* Translated by John A. Spaulding and George Simpson. New York: Free Press.
Eitzen, Stanley D., and George H. Sage. 2009. *Sociology of North American sport.* Boulder, CO: Paradigm Publishers.
Hirschi, Travis. 1969. *Causes of delinquency.* Berkeley: University of California Press.
———. [1969] 2005. *Causes of delinquency.* New Brunswick: Transaction Publishers.

Kornhauser, Ruth R. 1978. *Social sources of delinquency: An appraisal of analytic models*. Chicago: University of Chicago Press.

Lin, Nan. 1986. Conceptualizing social support. In *Social support, life events, and depression*, ed. Nan Lin, Alfred Dean, and William Ensel, 17-30. Orlando: Academic Press.

Lovell-Troy, Lawrence A. 1983. Anomia among employed wives and housewives: An exploratory analysis. *Journal of Marriage and the Family* 45: 301-310.

Lowry, Tom. 2003. The NFL machine. *Business Week*, January 27.

Lukes, Steven. 1972. *Emile Durkheim: His life and work*. New York: Harper and Row.

MacCambridge, Michael. 2004. *America's game: The epic story of how pro football captured a nation*. New York: Random House.

MacIver, Robert M. 1950. *The ramparts we guard*. New York: Macmillan Co.

Marks, Stephen R. 1974. Durkheim's theory of anomie. *American Journal of Sociology* 80: 329-363.

McClosky, Herbert, and John H. Schaar. 1965. Psychological dimensions of anomy. *American Sociological Review* 30: 14-40.

Merton, Robert K. 1938. Social structure and anomie. *American Sociological Review* 3: 672-682.

———. 1968. *Social theory and social structure*. New York: Free Press.

Messner, Steven, and Richard Rosenfeld. 1994. *Crime and the American dream*. Belmont, CA: Wadsworth.

Mestrovic, Stjepan G., and Helene M. Brown. 1985. Durkheim's concept of anomie as dereglement. *Social Problems* 33: 81-99.

Orru, Marco. 1987. *Anomie: History and meanings*. Boston: George Allen & Unwin.

Park, Robert, and Earnest Burgess. 1921. *Introduction to the science of sociology*. Chicago: University of Chicago Press.

Parsons, Talcott. 1937. *The structure of social action*. New York: McGraw Hill.

———. [1937] 1968. *The structure of social action*. New York: Free Press.

Passas, Nikos. 2000. Continuities in the anomie tradition. In *The legacy of anomie theory*, ed. Freda Adler and William S. Laufer, 91-112. New Brunswick, NJ: Transaction Publishers.

Pope, Whitney. 1976. *Durkheim's Suicide*. Chicago: University of Chicago Press.

Powell, Elwin H., ed. 1970. *The design of discord: Studies of anomie.* New York: Oxford University Press.
Riesman, David, Nathan Glazer, and Revel Denney. 1956. *The lonely crowd: A study in the changing American character.* New York: Doubleday & Company.
Srole, Leo. 1956. Social integration and certain corollaries: An exploratory study. *American Sociological Review* 21: 709-716.
Sutherland, Edwin H. 1947. *Principles of criminology.* 4th ed. Philadelphia: Lippincott.
Sutherland, Edwin H., Donald R. Cressey, and David F. Luckenbill. 1992. *Principles of criminology.* 11th ed. Dix Hills, NY: General Hall.
Thompson, Kenneth. 1982. *Emile Durkheim.* New York: Tavistock Publications.
Thorlindsson, Thorolfur. 1983. Social organizations and cognition. *Human Development* 26: 289-307.
Thorlindsson, Thorolfur and Thoroddur Bjarnason. 1998. Modeling Durkheim on the micro level: A study of youth suicidality. *American Sociological Review* 63: 94-110.
USA Today. 2007. What is the average salary of an NFL football player? < http://asp.usatoday.com/sports/football/nfl/salaries/median salaries.aspx?year=2007 >. Retrieved June 24, 2008.
Vaux, Alan. 1988. *Social support: Theory, research, and intervention.* New York: Praeger.
Vold, George B., and Thomas J. Bernard. 1986. *Theoretical criminology.* New York: Oxford University Press.
Wirth, Louis. 1951. Preface to *Ideology and utopia: An introduction to the sociology of knowledge*, by Karl Mannheim, xxv. New York: Harcourt Brace.
Whannel, Garry. 2002. *Media sport stars: Masculinities and moralities.* London: Routledge.
Wolfgang, Marvin E., and Franco Ferracuti. 1967. *The subculture of violence.* London: Tavistock Publishers.
Wright, John Paul. 1996. Unpublished manuscript. Parental support and delinquent behavior: The limits of control theory. Chicago: American Society of Criminology.
Wright, John Paul, Francis T. Cullen, and John D. Wooldredge. 1995. Unpublished manuscript. Parental support and juvenile delinquency: A social capital approach. Boston: American Society of Criminology.

Yost, Mark. 2006. *Tailgating, sacks, and salary caps: How the NFL became the most successful sports league in history*. Chicago: Kaplan Publishing.

Chapter Three

Accessing the Lives of Professional Football Players: Stories Revealed

The study for this book was conceptualized and designed after many personal conversations and in-depth interviews with two former NFL players and has evolved over a five-year period. Initially, elite and specialized interviews (Dexter 1970) provided insight and opportunity to conceptualize a qualitative approach based on inductive techniques, which has been termed "field research or naturalistic research" by Schatzman and Strauss (1973) in their text, *Field Research: Strategies for a Natural Sociology*. Later I determined that more data and comparable data could be obtained by developing a structured interview guide that could be administered or self-administered by players. The second phase of research allowed for a more deductive approach based on the findings of the qualitative/naturalistic field data and on social disorganization theory.

The blended form of research (Creswell 2005; Jick 1979), which first began as an open-ended inquiry and qualitative field research, then formed into a quantitative format that allowed for a more comprehensive look into the lives of NFL players. The qualitative data help reveal "qualities" of behavior that could be missed from a purely quantitative approach (Strauss 2003). The structured interview guide, composed of sixty variables designed from theory and the inductive data, yields additional comparative data. The closed nature of a professional sports league such as the NFL begs the use of this blended method to maximize data on the players.

Entering the Field

The first step in the qualitative research process was gaining access to NFL players. Elite and specialized interviewing was employed as a way to gain access to two former NFL players. These two players became "key informants," and the point of entry for gaining access to other players. Lewis Dexter (1970) suggests the applicability and use of this approach for closed, influential, and prominent populations. In essence, elite interviewing, as defined by Dexter (1970), means that the investigator "is willing, and often eager to let the interviewee teach him what the problem, the question, the situation, is—to the limits, of course, of the interviewer's ability to perceive relationships to his basic problems, whatever these may be" (6).

Dexter's thorough description of elite and specialized interviewing makes the point that in many cases the use of "well informed" persons or informants is the only way to gain entrance into select groups. According to Paul (1953), key informants are,

> ideally . . . individuals who have not only proved themselves well informed and well connected, but have demonstrated a capacity to adopt the standpoint of the investigator. Informing him of rumors and coming events, suggesting secondary informants, preparing the way, advising on tactics and tact, securing additional data on their own, and assisting the anthropologist in numerous other ways. (430)

Concentration on relatively few informants for this book helped me acquire a better picture of the norms, attitudes, expectations, and values of the players under study than typically could be obtained solely from larger numbers of less intensive interviews. However, Dexter (1970) notes, ". . . it will often be preferable to combine the use of informants with other interviewing and with other methods of data collection" (8-9).

A second major step in the qualitative research process was movement beyond the two initial informants to the larger "field" of NFL players. In order to accomplish this methodological step, I relied upon Schatzman and Strauss's (1973) classic work on field research and Strauss's (2003) work on qualitative analysis. Central to the Schatzman and Strauss paradigm are several important processes. These include: (1) entering; (2) organizing; (3) watching; (4) recording; and (5) analyzing. Each of these can be simultaneous data collection activities and are essential in understanding the qualities of the behavior under investigation. Schatzman and Strauss emphasized the emergent nature of human behavior and that qualitative research must remain open to new and continuing questions in order to capture the truly natural essence of human behavior. Strauss illustrates the various methods available to discover points of commonality and difference within qualitative data. Much of his emphasis on analysis is based on organization and thematic commonalities. Figure 1 illustrates the phases of qualitative data collection as based on the work of Dexter (1970), Schatzman and Strauss (1973), and Strauss (2003).

Figure 1: Qualitative Research Process— Phases of Data Collection

Step 1
Entrée via key informants, two former NFL players with significant experience having played on several teams. A detailed description of life in the NFL for the informants and their peers (research method: elite and specialized interviews, Dexter 1970).

↓

Step 2
Access to other NFL players via connections made through informants. Further interviewing and observation beyond the initial two informants (research method: field work, Schatzman and Strauss 1973).

↓

Step 3
Organizing and analyzing field data into themes and categories such as: (1) Deviance/Law-Breakers; (2) Rapid Life Change: The Presence of Anomie; and (3) The Importance of Social Ties/Support (research method, Schatzman and Strauss 1973; Strauss 2003).

↓

Step 4
Posing the research questions and developing generalized observations across the themes and categories via the qualities demonstrated during the field research (research method, Strauss 2003).

Step One: My First Glimpse

From 2001 to 2006, I engaged in fieldwork in several locations, which were rich with "NFL communities." The motivation for this fieldwork came almost simultaneously with conceptualizing a research project on professional sport and conversations with a friend who happened to be a former NFL player. I then began to reflect on earlier conversations with another friend, also a former NFL player. I began to read and explore much of the available literature on professional sports and deviance (e.g., Benedict 1997; Benedict & Yaeger 1998; Blumstein & Benedict 1999; Starr & Samuels 2000). The literature is rich with examples of athletes who find themselves in trouble with the law. However, most of the literature is journalistic in nature. I found very few explanations for deviant behavior. With the literature and these formerly mentioned intimate conversations fresh in memory, I began to think about and conceptualize a study on the NFL and its players. It was apparent that explanations other than journalistic were needed. At times, even the questions in the contemporary literature were not very clear.

My first real glimpse into the NFL came as a result of numerous intimate personal conversations with a former NFL player back in 1997. This was several years before I would even be considering any form of research, much less a book; yet those in-depth conversations held the key to the evolving study. This former player, whom I will refer to as John,[1] had just retired from the NFL at the time of our initial conversations.

At that time, he appeared to still be in impeccable physical condition not to mention relatively young. This observation led me to ask him why he had retired when it appeared he had several more productive years left to play, particularly since his production the last year he played was above average for players at his position. This question prompted John to disclose many stories about the deviant behaviors of players he knew. He described a series of destructive lifestyles he and others had indulged in and the deviant life-choices that came as a result—the promiscuous sex, daily drug use, alcohol abuse, domestic abuse, rapes, attempted suicides, and so on. He referred to many of these behaviors as reasons why he had ended his professional career. His frequent run-ins with the law and a court-ordered rehabilitation essentially forced him into retirement. His stories left an impression and prompted more questions and then even more questions about how this happens to a gifted and talented young professional.

This real life case did not seem rational to me. Here was a great athlete, who had made millions of dollars, who had everything most Americans can only dream of, who had his career cut short because he could not stay out of jail. This seemed to be a cruel paradox. As we visited for several weeks, John told me many incredible stories. At the end of our last conversation in 1997, I finally asked if there was a reason why he was unable to curb his unlawful behavior. I remember exactly what he told me: "I was instantly rich, and I couldn't handle it."

A few years later, I was re-introduced to Soloman (another former NFL player, a friend that I had not seen since childhood). As a young boy, I had the privilege of knowing Soloman when he played football at the college where my father was employed. As a young football fan, I looked up to Soloman for his athletic prowess and status as an all-American collegiate football player. For a short time, Soloman took me under his wing and explained the intricacies of the game of football, escorted me around the locker room, took me to other various social events, and explained the process of "making it to the NFL," at a time when he was being scouted by numerous NFL teams.

In 2000, I met Soloman at a hotel in the Midwest to catch up and hear about his career in the NFL. When the topic turned from family and friends to the NFL, he started describing the wild, deviant, and unlawful behaviors/activities that he had witnessed—descriptions of behaviors that reminded me of earlier conversations with John. After Soloman told me about a good friend in the league who had just tried to kill himself, I asked myself how athletes who had "everything" could end up in this condition? This question would become the topic and problem of the research for this book.

Step Two: Becoming One of the "Boys": Access to Additional Stories

Several months later, while visiting John in Texas, I began to develop ideas for a more extensive project. John took me to many of the local establishments where professional athletes "hung out." Later, John, who still had numerous friends in the league, took me to a Sunday night game. We had front row seats for the game and were subsequently escorted to the field where he introduced me to several players. The following day, John took me to meet many of the players I had met after the game. At this point, I realized that I had gained access to an affluent, elite, yet seemingly delinquent and closed, social group.

My observation of these athletes revealed that many of them were very cynical and wary of outsiders, a fact that cannot be overstated. Most have been "burned" (mistreated or lied to) on numerous occasions by journalists, reporters, agents, and even friends. They were very aware of these "outsiders" and their frequently exploitive intentions. It was only through my informants that initial, but skeptical, access was gained. Once I had gained initial access and my informants had told their peers numerous times that I was "okay" and could be considered one of the "boys," the other players began to feel more at ease and started to open up to me. I told them that I was doing research on NFL players' activities off the field and wanted to get the inside view of what goes on in their lives and the NFL. I also kept reiterating that everything they did in my presence and told me would be confidential and not used to harm them in any way. I emphasized that I was interested in the group characteristics and not one player per se.

They began to view me in a unique way. Although some called me "professor," at the same time I was becoming one of the "boys," ultimately the most important distinction I could acquire from the players. Without being labeled as such, I undoubtedly, would have been categorized with the media and other reporters, and viewed as someone, as one player told me, who was "just out to get the most recent and juiciest gossip." I think, in many ways, after some initial conversation, they felt we had some "things in common"—especially a love for athletics, in particular football. They were impressed that I'd "done my homework" and knew about their professional careers, statistics, and the game of football in general. Also, on many occasions, I played golf and basketball with some of the players, which ultimately expanded my access and legitimized me. My being able to hang out with these athletes really helped them begin to feel comfortable with me and opened a lot of doors for further access.

Most seemed to enjoy talking to me and viewed me as knowledgeable—someone they could confide in, as most did not feel they could with their agents, reporters, or even other peers. They appeared to appreciate my role as the "professor" and even at times told me that what I was doing was important in that they could talk about the many problems they faced as celebrities and professional athletes. These interviews highlighted that need—one which the players themselves regarded as an important issue.

As I continued my conversations with John and Soloman, interviews with other players began to snowball. The initial relationships I had built were now paying off. The players that I interviewed in Texas, as well as my two informants, began to tell their peers that I was "okay" and that they should "help me out" with my research. Some even told other players that I was someone they could talk to about personal issues they were dealing with and that maybe I could help. As these interviews unfolded and I tried to understand their situations, I could feel their respect and desire to assist me in understanding the real life situations they find themselves in as NFL players.

In summer of the following year (2001), having received an all-access pass, I was permitted to attend an NFL training camp. This access came with the help of an individual who had ties to this NFL team. I was able to talk with the head coach and a couple of front office officials about my research. Subsequently, I was introduced to numerous players during their breaks, many of whom granted me interviews. These conversations also led to interviews with other players later that year. Many of these further interviews were also facilitated by my two informants. This, alongside my fieldwork in Texas earlier in the year, was the beginning of my interviewing, which continued through the week of the 2005 Super Bowl.

That week was the last of my significant data collection periods for this study. It was during this experience, when Soloman and I walked unchallenged through the intense security, police, police dogs, and huge numbers of hotel staff into one of the team hotels and into a secure location where only the players, coaches, intimate others, and select media were allowed, that I knew there was something special and rare about the kind of access I had gained. Soloman almost immediately started introducing me to players and coaches. These conversations turned into in-depth interviews later in the week.

These in-depth interviews were largely unstructured, open-ended, and based on prior elite and specialized interviewing with John and Soloman. The strength of this type of interview is that it collects descriptive data in a very natural method (Schatzman & Strauss 1973). Later, I began to ask more difficult questions as my level of comfort grew. In this study, I asked about the athlete's world in order to draw out a description of their activities, routines, and relationships. These kinds of questions helped draw out data descriptive of the *life experiences* of the athletes.

I typically opened the in-depth interviews with several general questions or statements such as: "Tell me about yourself"; "where did you go to school?"; "where's home?" In other words, I asked them to tell me about the various stages of their life (childhood through college) leading up to the NFL. I also asked them about changes they had experienced en route to becoming a professional football player. Finally I asked them to tell me about life in the NFL. I frequently found myself engaged in conversations about their family, wealth, being a celebrity, their happiness or unhappiness, drug and alcohol abuse, promiscuous sexual conduct, and criminal or unlawful behavior. During this phase, as my acceptance level grew and as I became more comfortable, I began to use the questionnaire. The data collection from the questionnaire will be discussed in chapter 7.

Of the 104 NFL players interviewed during this five-year period, most mentioned the presence of deviant lifestyles and the range of concerns that result from being suddenly wealthy. Many said they were unable to cope with the freedom that came with sudden wealth and fame. At times, I was almost overwhelmed by the litany of chronic personal and social problems these players had experienced. They described the role that prior socialization and social support—or lack of them—played in their lives.

Step Three: Organizing and Analyzing the Stories

The discussion is based on three *core themes* that emerged from the qualitative data: (a) deviant behaviors, activities, and lifestyles; (b) anomie (sudden life changes in status and wealth); and (c) the importance of social ties and support. Using an inductive approach, I was interested ". . . not in the viewpoints of specific individuals but in the general patterns [or themes] evinced by classes of individuals" (Strauss 1987: 268) or, in terms of this study, evinced by a group of athletes (with commonalities) caught up in "the NFL lifestyle." Many players suggested that they, and their peers, were subject to varied sets of social dynamics, socialization experiences, and family structures and that certain social ties and support factors had profound effects on their lives, their behavioral patterns, and their ability to cope with life, status, and economic change (most importantly sudden and extreme wealth). Figure 2 illustrates the major themes evidenced from the qualitative data.

Figure 2: A Working Behavioral and Attitudinal Model for NFL Players Derived From Field Study

Major Themes which Emerged Across the Sample of NFL Players		
(1) *Evidence of Deviance*	(2) *Indications of Anomie*	(3) *Social Ties*
Factors Influencing Themes		
Deviance as Demonstrated by: • Law Breaking Behavior • Evading Arrests because of Police Deference • Deviance without Arrests • Receiving Rehabilitation or Counseling	Anomie as Demonstrated by: • Reactions to Sudden Wealth and Status Change • Unhappiness and the Search for Meaning and Life Satisfaction	Institutions and Social Networks that Provide Social Support/Control: • Strength of Marriage • Extent of Family Structure • Level of Educational Background • Presence of Practicing Religion • Peer Network Early Socialization • Childhood Family Dynamics • Socioeconomic Status • Urban/Rural Location • Childhood Friends

Note

1. All names of places and individuals have been changed to protect the anonymity of the study's participants.

References

Benedict, Jeff. 1997. *Public heroes, private felons*. Boston: Northeastern University Press.

Benedict, Jeff, and Don Yaeger. 1998. *Pros and cons: The criminals who play in the NFL*. New York: Warner Books.

Blumstein, Alfred, and Jeff Benedict. 1999. Criminal violence of NFL players compared to the general population. *Chance* 12: 12-15.

Creswell, John W. 2005. *Educational research: Planning, conducting, and evaluating quantitative and qualitative research*. Upper Saddle River, NJ: Pearson.

Dexter, Lewis A. 1970. *Elite and specialized interviewing*. Evanston: Northwestern University Press.

Jick, Todd. 1979. Mixing qualitative and quantitative methods: Triangulation in action. *Administrative Science Quarterly* 24: 602-611.

Paul, Benjamin D. 1953. Interview techniques and field relationships. In *Anthropology Today*, ed. A. L. Kroeber, 430-451. Chicago: University of Chicago Press.

Schatzman, Leonard, and Anselm L. Strauss. 1973. *Field research: Strategies for a natural sociology*. Englewood Cliffs, NJ: Prentice-Hall.

Strauss, Anselm L. 1987. *Qualitative analysis for social scientists*. Cambridge: Cambridge University Press.

———. [1987] 2003. *Qualitative analysis for social scientists*. New York: Cambridge University Press.

Chapter Four

Illegal Procedure: Seeing Patterns of Deviance

Typically, the interviews revealed that deviance, which consisted of unlawful behavior or other erratic behaviors, transpired in relation to the life change that occurred when players entered the NFL from college. More importantly, the suddenly acquired wealth that came with this life change, appeared to be a key factor in the NFL players' propensity for deviance. Put simply, the money that players were exposed to allowed them to pursue behavior and activities that, under previous circumstances, many could not afford. The money allowed for excess levels of almost anything a player wanted. Many times, these excesses led to deviant and illegal activities. Figure 1 shows the categories of deviant behavior within the overarching theme.

Figure 1: Deviance Theme

Deviance, Commonalities in NFL Players' Language:

"*my wrongdoings, delinquent, terrible, bad, corrupt, shame, flawed, defective, immoral, consumed, consequences, addicted, abuse, sin*"

Categories:
- Law Breaking Behavior
- Evading Arrests because of Police Deference
- Deviance without Arrests
- Rehabilitation/Counseling

Law Breaking Behavior

In many cases, deviant behaviors turned into unlawful or illegal actions. A number of players reported having been arrested after entering the NFL for anything from illegal drug possession, to soliciting prostitutes, to drinking and driving, to rape, to assault. A key pattern for law breakers appeared to revolve around money and power issues. Many of the players that had been arrested told me that their wealth and power had been a stimulus and a driving force for their unlawful activities. I would argue that their wealth provided them a platform from which to deviate. In essence, many had difficulty coping with sudden affluence and the situations that wealth created. The sense of entitlement that came with wealth gave many of the athletes the idea that they only answered to themselves and that there were few consequences for their behavior.

Moreover, I found that much of the players' sense of entitlement was a result of being seen as famous and, to some extent, was perpetuated by team owners and management. Much deviance and even illegal behaviors were, or appeared to be, condoned by team owners and management. While owners and management are very concerned about team image, they are dealing daily with players and problems. From their perspective, players come and go. Football is a business. Winning is good for business. Hence, better players with questionable behavior are tolerated up to a point, especially if public relation damage control stays within an acceptable level determined by the team management.

For example, I was told of one instance in which fourteen NFL players were accused of sexual misconduct. The players involved offered the accuser a large sum of money in order for her not to go to the police. The owner of the team was notified of these allegations and immediately called for a private meeting with two of his star players who were involved in the incident. According to one of these players, the owner said, "I don't know if you all did it or didn't do it, and I don't want to." He went on to give the players the phone number of a lawyer who "could take care of it" for them.

In essence, these players' destructive behaviors appear to have been ignored by team management. The owner commented later, according to one of the players involved, "If this was simply a consensual orgy, I'm not all that concerned. . . . There is no reason to consider suspension." Eventually, the players involved, facilitated by the organization, paid off the accuser, as reported by the player. There were no consequences for the players involved—even after several had admitted that they had indeed been involved in the "nonconsensual" sexual orgy. Even though this incident did not result in the filing of official charges, twelve of these fourteen players involved in the sexual misconduct were eventually arrested and charged with various other illegal activities. In terms of the accuser, she was demonized for seeking compensation and legal representation. This was a classic case of "blaming the victim," something, one player told me, many pro athletes become skilled at. I would argue that the appearance of "no consequences" in this case gave these athletes a sense of limitless boundaries. If there were clearer, established boundaries, some consequences, or more importantly support programs in place, perhaps some of the players would have changed their behavior. Nonetheless, these kinds of crimes against women are shocking and emphasize a larger systemic issue surrounding privileged celebrity athletes and those who enable their deviant behavior.

In essence, the message from many of the players interviewed seemed to be that if you are a professional football player you are entitled to do as you wish without the threat of "harsh" consequences or any corrective social support from your team. This sense of entitlement empowered by wealth and status, appeared to be a key factor in players' illegal behaviors. The phrases below are quotes from the players. They are typical comments that I heard across interview settings.

> Marshall: I never seemed to have enough, enough women, enough dope . . . [eventually] *I got busted*.
>
> Chris: *I've been arrested* several times . . . you see, I thought I was above the law . . . and consequences, I never thought about consequences.
>
> Eric: *I been arrested* . . . got into a bar fight and was busted for possession.
>
> Aaron: I got into some rough shit, man . . . too much money and free time. . . . Usually, I could find a way out . . . but last year *I got taken in* [arrested].
>
> Jay: Things changed so damn fast. . . . I started to use alcohol to take the edge off. . . . *I've been arrested* several times, hell, I've had three DUIs.

Dave: If you play in this league . . . it's a fast-paced world . . . and a lot of these young men use alcohol and drugs to cope with their new lifestyle, I've known so many that have been *arrested* numerous times.

Jerry: I didn't know how to turn all this stuff down . . . I never had any of it growing up . . . the money, man, the money, I couldn't handle it . . . I started blowing it on all sorts of shit . . . next thing I know *I'm in jail* for solicitation [of a prostitute].

Will: *I've been arrested* twice on drug charges.

Jonathan: You get involved in the nightlife . . . you gonna get in trouble . . . I consider myself lucky, only being *cuffed* [arrested] once . . . I had to get out . . . it would've killed me.

Nate: My life, man, it's a fucking wreck. . . . *I've now been arrested* four goddamn times.

Evading Arrests because of Police Deference

Even if some of the players in the sample were not physically arrested and charged with an illegal offense (as in the case of the fourteen players mentioned above), many continued to engage in unlawful acts with their status as professional football players affording them, as one NFL player told me, "a free pass." In other words, the police and other authorities "permitted" athletes to participate in illegal activities without subjecting them to arrest. Police refused to arrest and others refused to press charges against many of the athletes because they deferred to their status as NFL players. This led me to conclude that if we count only arrested law breakers among them, we are likely underestimating the number of NFL players involved in illegal behavior. As one player told me, "If you have enough money and people know who you are, you can get out of just about anything." Below are common phrases that describe situations in which players were not arrested after they had been involved in illegal activities and had been stopped or confronted by police.

Marcus: *I should've ended up in jail* . . . but, I was simply slapped on the wrist and told not to do it again.

James: I don't even know how many times I've had run-ins with the law . . . its more than a couple . . . but every time *I somehow seemed to escape* the consequences of my actions.

Demetrius: If you're a pro athlete, a lot of times *you can get away with* murder, just look at [a notable NFL player] . . . in some ways, it's like there are no rules as long as we can perform on Sunday.

Matt: I've been stopped by the cops several times . . . thought I was done . . . I had been drinking and had a bag [marijuana] in the car . . . but once the cop found out who I was, he told me to go on . . . I signed a couple of autographs for him and he forgot it . . . so *I ended up getting off*.

Danny: I knew the law wouldn't touch me . . . and they didn't . . . Throughout my career *I've been able to get off* more time than not.

Mike: In the . . . NFL, everyone's vulnerable, *they just don't all get caught* or held accountable.

Alan: When *these guys get off so easily* . . . all of the time . . . you see, this is what promotes and even perpetuates even more of these kinds of actions . . . the drinking and driving, buying hookers, beating wives and girlfriends, and all that kind of shit.

Dwight: And people wonder why these young men got the god-complex . . . because, hell, *they can usually get away with* whatever the fuck they want . . . and this ain't good.

Deviance without Arrests

Many of the players also reported participating in many other forms of deviant or erratic behaviors, behaviors that were not all strictly illegal (some of these behaviors may be illegal in some places, but are not always regularly investigated or prosecuted). These behaviors included spending large sums of money on sex (strip/gentleman clubs) and substances (alcohol and drugs), promiscuous and unusual sex with multiple partners, alcohol abuse, domestic abuse, drug abuse, and suicide attempts. According to many of the players in this category, their wealth and status set the stage for many of their deviant behavioral outcomes. As one player told me, "We make a lot of money . . . that's our lifestyle . . . it sets us up for crazy, kinky shit." Another player told me, "You go to a club, they treat you like a king . . . you get escorted to the VIP suite, they bring you Don Perignon and strawberries . . . everything is on the house, even the women." This type of "VIP" treatment appeared to be associated with player deviance. Below are common phrases that outline several of these deviant behaviors and activities.

> Dallas: You see, fame works two ways, I'll pay you and then you pay me . . . the *drugs* were killing me.

> Terry: *This life* was starting to slowly kill me . . . I've blown thousands of dollars in bars, strip clubs . . . and . . . the *crazy sex* with many, many women . . . you'd think with this kind of freedom I would be happy, I wasn't.

> Michael: My thing was sex, *sex* with tons of women . . . I didn't discriminate, but *this kind of life* was killing me.

> Marcus: I could talk about the *gang bangs*, the *drug abuse*, and on and on.

> Antwan: We think the more we have the better we gonna feel, the more *steroids* we pump the better we gonna feel, the more women we fuck the cooler we gonna be . . . there just ain't no end, and its . . . tiring . . . so what do we do, more *drugs*, more *sex*, more *liquor*.

> Jimmy: Damn, we've been involved in some kinky shit . . . the bizarre *sex*, the *drugs*.

> Rob: I don't know how many guys I know that *beat women*, their wives or their girlfriends, or for that matter, both . . . it seems to be a common thing.

Lawrence: It seems like, every week, one of my teammates is involved in a bar room *brawl*. . . . *They get drunk* and do stupid shit. . . . I've even been involved in a few of them.

Jerry: One of my boys, man, he got so depressed and fucked up on *drugs*, he *tried to kill himself*.

Chad: You wouldn't think it . . . and its covered up a lot . . . *guys trying to kill themselves* . . . *suicide attempts* are more frequent than anyone would think.

Rehabilitation/Counseling

Although I typically would not label rehabilitation or counseling a deviant behavior, it was included within this theme because rehabilitation, in many cases, was an outcome of the deviant actions of NFL players in my study group. In the interviews, many players said they needed to get help or some sort of counseling for various addictions and personal troubles. I concluded from the qualitative data that those individuals who had received counseling or rehabilitation were, in most cases, involved in unlawful or illegal activities. Below are some common phrases that highlight the situations in which NFL players found themselves and in which rehabilitation or counseling was necessary.[1]

Gordon: I got injured back in [a date] . . . started taking pain killers . . . *I got hooked* and was forced to go to a *rehabilitation facility*.

Adam: After my third DUI, they made me check into *rehab* . . . *I was hooked* on some bad shit.*

Aaron: I was into so much shit, coke, dope, a bunch of shit, I didn't know if I was comin' or goin' . . . I been to different *rehabs* five times now . . . it took awhile to realize *how hooked I was*.*

Mike: In order to keep my license I had to get some substance abuse *counseling* . . . I had to finally admit to myself that *I was hooked*.*

Todd: It happened so fast, it was like, fuck, the lifestyle got hold of me . . . and it took a long time for me to understand *my addiction*, I had to go to *rehab*.

Many of the players' comments revealed that deviance (illegal or legal) was connected to wealth and the athletes' newfound status as professional football players. A sense of entitlement appeared to influence the ability of many players to make, what I would describe as mature, adult life-choice decisions. Time and time again, abrupt life and economic change seemed to be an important factor in terms of their participation in deviant behaviors and activities. There also appeared to be a relationship between those who had received counseling/rehabilitation and those who were involved in illegal activities. Nearly every player that had received counseling/rehabilitation had also been arrested.

In essence, players reporting involvement in deviant behavior also made reference to their wealth and status. This was a finding that cannot be highlighted enough. In many cases, players told me that a majority of their deviance was only possible because they had the appropriate resources (money and status). And, interestingly, many of the players felt that they had the "right" to do as they pleased simply because of their fame and recognition as a professional athlete. Also, many stated that the lack of consequences for their actions perpetuated further deviance. Thus, I would conclude that their perceived empowerment from wealth and fame, as well as the absence of meaningful social control and support mechanisms (team organizations and law enforcement) were important factors in regard to furthering their behavior into more social deviance.

Ideal-Typical Deviance

During a conversation at a sports bar in Texas with several players, Shaun told me an unfortunate story of deviant and unlawful behavior in which he was involved. After I reviewed the qualitative data, this story appeared to represent a common pattern of deviance among the players in the sample. To me, this appeared to be an "ideal type" since it was a situation that could be revisited in the lives of many NFL players.

Shaun explained to me that he and another star millionaire NFL player had decided to blow off some steam after the season back in the late 1990s. They rented a suite at a local hotel. Through some connections the players had with a local gentleman's club, they invited three topless dancers to their suite. After spending some time "getting to know one another," or in other words, smoking several cocaine laced joints and having a few cocktails, the two players encouraged the women to have sex with each other. The two players gave the women several objects typically used for sexual stimulation. "We sat back and told the bitches what we wanted them to do . . . they did it," Shaun told me. He also said that this was not out of the ordinary, that they and "everyone I know" takes part in similar deviant activities. They continued the evening by engaging in group sex, doing cocaine, smoking marijuana, and drinking heavily.

This scenario continued for three consecutive days, until finally the hotel manager became suspicious of prostitution. The manager informed the local authorities of his suspicion and the five individuals were arrested and charged, not with prostitution or solicitation, but with illegal drug possession. Eventually, the charges were dropped.

This story, along with the many other similar accounts I heard about drug abuse and wild promiscuous sexual behavior was a prevalent and reoccurring theme from the qualitative data. To me, these stories revealed that as these NFL players' gained wealth and status, their behavioral license expanded, which created increased opportunities for deviance to occur. These accounts indicated that, in many cases, women became sexual prey for these athletes in which their self-gratifying deviance turned into illegal behaviors. This deviance was then dismissed by the athletes, as well as, law enforcement and the NFL, as minor, isolated incidents. As one player told me, "boys will always be boys."

Note

1. An asterisk indicates that the player from whom the quote came was arrested after entering the NFL.

Chapter Five

Out of Bounds: Seeing Patterns of Anomie

Another common theme that emerged from the interviews was that most of the players reported difficulty with life change, in particular, sudden wealth. One finding that surprised me was that many players in my study group reported being unhappy with life. Several went as far to say that they felt their life was meaningless. Figure 1 shows the categories of anomic behavior.

Figure 1: Anomie Theme

Anomie, Commonalities in NFL Players' Language:

"life changes, world changed, change, suddenly transformed, sudden, gratification, intensified, loss of self-control, transformation, entitlement, meaningless, chaotic, fast-paced, hard times, unhappy, unhappiness, out of control, cope, trying to cope"

Categories:
- Sudden Wealth and Status Change
- Happy verses Unhappy with Life

Sudden Wealth and Status Change

Many of the NFL players in the sample talked about their inability to cope with sudden life, status, and economic change. Numerous players referred to life in the NFL as incredibly "fast-paced" or the "NFL lifestyle." A common pattern among players was that without support, "this lifestyle" will eventually "kill you."

For this study, this point cannot be overstated. The data revealed that with many of the players' transition from college to the NFL, change was "sudden"—especially regarding wealth. In college, the majority of these players were scholarship athletes that had some level of support and structure. But they were, in most cases, not permitted by the NCAA to work or accept any outside funds. With many of the athletes coming from very humble families or households, there was little financial support for the athletes from their parents or guardians (families). Therefore most were forced to remain in relative "poverty" until they were drafted or signed by an NFL team (or signed with an agent). Thus, going from unpaid student-athletes to, in many cases, millionaires, was a sudden and violent life change. Below are common phrases that illustrate some of the anomic conditions and characteristics of the players.[1]

> Shawn: A lot of these athletes think they are bigger than life now. . . . Shit, I did. *My life changed* so fucking fast, I was a fucking star.

> Joey: You begin to think you're some type of god . . . *your life changes*, you've got money, people know who you are, fuck, man, that shit goes to your head.*

> Robbie: We were given everything . . . and now you think you can do anything and get away with it . . . It's like, isn't that what they say, you have the world in the palm of your hand, and *it happens so damn fast*.

> Nate: Guys were given everything . . . *I had everything just like that*.

> Paul: For a while man, I thought I was bigger than life itself. . . . How could I not? *I had instant credibility*.

> Demetrius: Money, they say money is power and with money comes prestige . . . this is a change that I didn't handle very well . . . and most that I know didn't handle it well either. . . . It's

hard to when *your whole fucking world changes* right in front of your eyes.

Sammy: I realize now . . . before I went into the NFL, well, I never knew how to treat women and all that stuff, so once I was drafted by the [NFL team] *everything intensified* . . . now I had money . . . it didn't take long . . . I was out of fucking control.*

Happy verses Unhappy with Life

Contrary to common belief, an overwhelming number of the NFL players told me they were unhappy with some aspect of life. Most fans would think that athletes would have an extremely high rate of self-reported happiness. They are, after all, wealthy and famous. Yet, many were unhappy and felt that life (off the football field) was meaningless. A common pattern within this theme revealed that the extreme changes that occurred in their lives had a substantial effect on their level of happiness. Numerous players told me that sudden wealth did not bring stability and happiness, but an unexplainable dissatisfaction with their lives. I would argue that this "unexplainable" dissatisfaction may be what Durkheim described as *anomie*. Below are common phrases that highlight this finding.

Will: My life off the field, honestly, it's pretty . . . *meaningless.**

James: Everything changed around me . . . and everything seems chaotic . . . a lot of us, man, we *ain't even happy*, I ain't.

Lawrence: Really, we're a bunch of *deranged* motherfuckers.*

Chad: I thought with more championships and more honors, more money, more fame, more women, I would be able to find happiness . . . but, *I still felt empty.**

Adam: You got women everywhere, you still *ain't happy*, you got clothes and jewelry galore, you still *ain't happy*, you got pretty much everything you ever wanted, but you still *ain't happy* . . . How can a man who has everything be unhappy?

Eric: Right after I was drafted into the league . . . let me tell you about how *miserable* I really was inside.*

Cristian: I started to ask myself, *where can I find some happiness?*

Gerald: This ain't what I thought it was . . . *I'm not even happy.*

John: I had pretty much anything anybody could want, but *I wasn't all that happy* . . . that's pretty fucked up.*

David: I was so goddamn *unhappy.**

Perry: I had always thought I was a guy who had good judgment, good character . . . but, I kept finding myself doing crazy things . . . I thought, usually the next morning, damn, what the hell happened . . . I'm fucking *miserable* and out of control.*

Patrick: When I think back, there was really a sense of discontent in the locker room . . . almost like guys were really *unhappy* . . . with things outside of playing.

Alan: *Depression*, man, it runs rampant through the NFL.

Antwan: There's a lot of *miserable and unhappy* young men playing in this league . . . funny how being rich, famous, and athletically superior don't fulfill the soul.

Jay: The biggest change I see is that guys are making more and more money and what is required of them is so much less. They think they are bigger than life and the athletes today think they are above the law . . . and when all the cars and women lose their flavor, *misery* sets in and the bigger the money and glory gets, the more *miserable* a lot of these guys are.

In most cases it is easy to understand individuals' engaging in deviant activities when they are unhappy and feel that life is meaningless, especially during economic crises. But, it is more difficult to explain an increase in these states and behaviors during times of unusual economic prosperity. To their surprise, many of these athletes found sudden prosperity just as disastrous as sudden loss.

According to one player, "I never had nothin' my whole life, then I got drafted by the [NFL team], and I was, like, damn, now I'm rich . . .

and I was doing something I'd wanted to do my whole life." The problem was, as this player reflected further, "I had everything, just like that, I mean fucking everything . . . and ya'll all think that would be great, but I got bored, and when I was bored, I wasn't satisfied." He later told me that his personal life had become such a mess that he became bored with the one thing (football) that he had wanted to do his entire life. As he told me, "It got to the point where I even lost my love for the game, for football." He asked, "How could I get bored with money, beautiful women, being famous, and especially football? How could I get bored with all that shit? It's every man's dream. How the fuck could that happen?" These comments revealed to me an array of anomic characteristics. This athlete's anomic state later turned to deviance, with his being arrested on drug charges.

Thus, the field work revealed that, in many cases, rapid acquisition of wealth by NFL players appeared to result in states of unhappiness, in some cases meaninglessness, and in an array of deviant behaviors and activities. I would conclude that the data showed a pattern of association between the anomic characteristics of players and their propensity for social deviance.

Ideal-Typical Anomie

During a phone interview that was arranged by Soloman, Tyrone told me some of the intimate details of his almost tragic life story. This account appeared to represent a common pattern of anomie among the athletes in the study group. It was, I thought, the proto-typical story of an anomic individual.

Tyrone was raised by his grandmother in a public housing project located in a notoriously dangerous urban location. He managed to stay out of trouble (for the most part) while growing up by playing a variety of sports. In the early 1990s, he was chosen in the first round of the NFL draft. He signed a lucrative contract, making him one of the highest paid players at his position in NFL history. He later played for other NFL teams.

As he told me, he was determined to leave his humble past behind. He said, "I wanted to be rich." Then, in the midst of newfound affluence, he told me he was "transformed into a larger than life figure." He was now more than a professional football player, he was a celebrity. He got everything he wanted with the snap of a finger. He said, "I loved the sex—sex with many women. There weren't too many that I turned down. And the money. Briefly, my life was unbelievable. It was great." However, as he revealed, the more successful he became, the more he felt an unexplainable emptiness.

Along his path to fame, his dreams turned into nightmares. He told me, "The night we won [an important game], I was one of the first ones out of the locker room, probably the first one home and to bed, and I thought, this . . . this ain't what I thought it would be. I'm fucking miserable." But still, he thought with more football accolades, more wealth, more fame, more women, he would find what he was looking for, that ultimate happiness. The problem was that this happiness, he said, "wasn't there." He felt empty inside. According to one of his close friends, Tyrone's "ego was beginning to kill him." His wild behavior and promiscuous sexual pursuits cost him his family, and as he said, "my will to continue [live]." He told me over and over that he had everything, yet he was unhappy with his life. "I couldn't understand it," he kept repeating. Despite his wealth, fame, and athletic success, he was contemplating suicide.

Tyrone's account held many aspects (sudden wealth, fame, unhappiness, and deviance) that were common themes for many of the players in the study group. This was a story that was all too common for many of the players that I interviewed. Moreover, it revealed that many NFL players had difficulty coping with sudden wealth and status and that many, amid their confusion and unhappiness, resorted to deviant means to deal with the pressures of affluence and celebrity thrown at them by their high-profile profession.

Note

1. An asterisk indicates that the player from whom the quote came was arrested after entering the NFL.

Chapter Six

Inside the Huddle: Patterns of Social Support and Ties

The importance of common social ties or support structures such as marriage, family, education, religion, geographic location, and peer networks were common patterns in the interviews among the players. Many of these athletes revealed to me that those athletes integrated into, and regulated by, common social networks were more successful at coping with rapid change and affluence. Also, the qualitative data suggested that a number of the NFL players were subject to varied sets of social dynamics, socialization experiences, and family structures. In essence, some players had support while others did not. This seemed to contribute to either their happiness or unhappiness, and ultimately, their normative or deviant behavior. Thus, I would contend that these social ties/support factors surrounding "relationships" had a profound effect on the lives of many of these athletes, their behavioral patterns, and their ability to cope with social change—most importantly, sudden wealth. Figure 1 (on the following page) illustrates the key categories and subcategories that emerged within this theme.

Social Support/Control

From the interviews, social support/control factors emerged as important ties for the NFL players in the study. Among these factors were marriage and family, their level of education, religious beliefs, and networks of friends or peers. It appeared from the qualitative data that these factors had a buffering effect on stressful life change for many of the

Figure 1: Social Ties Theme

Social Ties, Commonalities in NFL Players' Language:

"link, tie, connection, higher connection, attachment, glue, bind, bond, support system, friendship, relationship"

Categories:	Sub-Categories:
Social Support/Social Control	• Marriage • Family structure • Educational background • Religion • Peer network
Early Socialization	• Childhood family dynamics • Socioeconomic status • Urban/Rural location • Childhood friends

players. As one player told me, "This kind of life [being a professional athlete] is hard enough with a very supportive family . . . if you take that away, it's almost impossible to keep your focus." In other words, without social support, many of these players coped with their newfound success through deviant means. But, when athletes experienced a stressful life event, such as entering the NFL (sudden wealth and status), social support (if available) was mobilized to mitigate the potentially pathological and/or negative consequences of the stressful/new experience. Moreover, it appeared that social support and control had buffering effects on deviance. Below are common examples (phrases) of these buffering qualities and illustration of further aspects of this theme.[1]

> Jeremy: You've got to have a *network* . . . you just don't know, you can't imagine, how important having a family or at least some true friends is . . . it gives you some limits . . . or at least makes you think twice . . . and, believe me, you need that . . . in this world it's too damn easy to get caught up in all kinds of shit that's gonna bring you down . . . *you need some support.*

Ruben: I was raised in one of the roughest places in [a Midwestern city], *people don't make it out without some kind of support.*

Marcus: My Dad . . . he's in prison . . . I had no one to teach me . . . *no one to offer me any support, and that's carried over to now.**

Tim: In the NFL, man, *you've got to have some support . . . without it you in trouble.**

Rob: *Support*, let me tell you, is a fucking necessity when you live this lifestyle.

Marriage

Todd: Being married . . . *kept me out of a lot of trouble.*

Dwight: I owe a lot to my wife . . . she *kept me on the straight and narrow.*

Sammy: A lot of times it don't matter [being married] . . . there's so many women . . . but I think it helps . . . those who are married seem to *have more of a foundation.*

Willie: After we *split up* [wife] . . . *all hell broke loose.**

Jordan: *My life was all fucked up after the divorce.* . . . I didn't realize how important my marriage was to my happiness.*

Family

Adam: *If I only had a father.**

Mike: I grew up with my mom and sister, but *not having a dad*, I had no male role model.*

Patrick: My Mom she brought me up . . . but *I didn't know my Dad.**

Freddy: *My Dad, I never knew him.**

Gus: If you're not rooted and grounded and have some sort of *structure like a family*, the NFL lifestyle will eventually consume you . . . and let me tell you sir, *these young men need their fathers*.

Educational Background

Ray: I wanted to be rich . . . to play at the next level, so I didn't really take school that seriously . . . looking back, though, *I really needed that foundation.**

Clinton: College . . . I didn't care, should have though, *it could've given me a strong foundation,* something to be proud of.*

Thomas: Didn't think about the importance of it [school] at the time, I wish I had . . . *I needed the support, the foundation* that it provided.

Chad: I wish I'd finished school . . . the guys that finish, don't take the quick money and go to the draft . . . it seems like they so much *better grounded* . . . I know it would have helped me, but I fucked up . . . if you really look at it, they the ones that seem to stay out of trouble, and be more productive and successful in all aspects of life.*

Jerry: Man, I needed to stay in school . . . I wasn't ready for all the shit that gets thrown at you, hell I just wasn't mature enough to make that kind of money yet, *I needed a much better foundation.**

Religion

Mark: The reason I got God . . . *I needed something bigger than myself* to grab a hold of . . . the pressures of playing pro football and being a celebrity and role model, they're great . . . and if you ain't got no family, no loving wife, or other things like that, its God . . . He's the only thing that's gonna save you.

Cheyenne: Having a relationship with Jesus . . . has literally saved my life, on so many occasions, through all the crazy shit that gets thrown at you . . . *I really needed something to live for*.

Marion: I got lucky . . . I was introduced to God . . . my life in shambles . . . *I needed something larger than myself* to believe in.

Aaron: Man, *that's garbage* [religion].*

John: *I don't need no god* . . . hell, I am one [although this was said jokingly, it seems to represent a common latent belief].*

Peers

Paul: *You'd think teammates would be supportive*, but when you know you're going to be playing against a guy next year, it's hard to be good friends with him . . . how can you be so close to someone you're supposed to hate?

Marshall: We ain't all friends, we're too selfish . . . we want to make the money while we can, hell man, it's survival of the fittest out there . . . I'll tell you, *there's not as much support* among players as you'd think.

Teddy: When you're trying to win [as a team] . . . and you have a guy like [a notable NFL player] just out for the money, it's hard to like him . . . or even respect him, that's why I think our *teammates aren't very good support*, and that's fucked up, man.

Chad: A lot of us just don't like each other, *there's no fucking real bond* there.*

Dave: Back in the day, man, most of us, we all got along, now it seems like *there's no support* of each other . . . we used to be in it together, but money, man, money is the root of all evil . . . now you see guys, they all burnt out and angry, for what though?

Early Socialization

According to the qualitative data, early socialization experiences and contexts appeared to also be a significant theme in the lives of many of the athletes. Key factors within this category that were frequently mentioned revolved around family dynamics and structure, where they were from, socioeconomic status, and their childhood friends/peers. The data suggested that growing up in a fractured family or a single parent/guardian household, particularly one lacking a father figure, had a variety of detrimental effects on many of the athletes. Alarmingly, many players reported having no connection to their biological father and a significant number also mentioned that their father was in prison. As one player told me, "so many of us never had a father figure, and just like in my case, mom worked twelve hours a day . . . I guess what I'm trying to say is this, that a lot of guys ain't got no clear definition of right and wrong, no male role model . . . they don't know how to make good decisions, I mean, I didn't, and it cost me." This player later said that he had had drug problems his entire NFL career. "I couldn't say no," he revealed over and over.

It was also apparent from the interviews that growing up in a densely populated area with many perceived social problems had a direct impact on many of their lives. According to one player, "when you go to sleep at night to sounds of gun shots right outside your bedroom, that stays with you, it affects you." Further, peer relationships appeared to be important as well. Another player, elaborating on the impact of insufficient social support, revealed that "some players in the league are great athletes, but they come from backgrounds where their families are absent so they join gangs or they've been around a lot of gang activity . . . [so] when this is your main support, let me say, good [life] choices don't happen." A number of players went on to talk about the damaging role gangs played in their early socialization. The data indicated that most players did not view gangs as a social support network.

Thus, players who were unable to maintain, or simply did not have, social ties for various reasons appeared to have more difficulty staying out of trouble. Also, many players reported that a close friend or family member had been shot, and some of them had died. Again, for many of the players in this study group, this represented an early socialization that was marred by poverty, a dangerous living environment, and the loss of those intimates that, perhaps, provided social bonds.

On the other hand, players who were raised in a more "traditional" family setting in a rural location appeared to have fewer problems later in life. The key to this finding, I would argue, is that support for players in this category largely came from having a father figure and, in essence, two parents/guardians.2 According to the data, these players had intimate relationships with family, and as one player said, "my parents taught me the difference between right and wrong . . . I had to abide by certain rules, I had boundaries and if I challenged those, there were consequences." Moreover, according to the interviews, those players that reported growing up in a more rural location typically mentioned that the town/city had a high level of religiosity. Many of the players told me that this was a key source of support for them. Some even mentioned the continued importance of the support they received from, not just their birth families, but from the churches they attended growing up. Below, common phrases illustrate and elaborate on this theme.

> Adrian: I was raised in a neighborhood so full of *crime* it came with its own fucking jail.*
>
> Michael: I grew up in South Carolina with just my Mom in a *public housing project*.*
>
> Karl: We were so *poor* . . . when I was a kid . . . my Mom she did the best she could, but she was never around . . . I guess I kind of raised myself.*
>
> Chris: My Mom and I lived in what I thought at the time was a normal family . . . hell, it was normal to be *poor* . . . but I look back, and think what a terrible existence, and my Dad, hell, I never knew him, I always despised him.
>
> Adam: I guess I always blamed my father for our *poverty* growing up . . . he involved in all kinds of shit, in and out of *jail*, he was a real fucking loser.*

Childhood Family Dynamics

> Jerry: Let me tell you, *I never had no relationship with my old man* . . . all I know is *I heard he was in the pen* . . . what a fuckup.*

Jamal: I grew up in a place so dangerous you wouldn't believe . . . and the drugs in our neighborhood, I don't even know if you could even call it a neighborhood . . . I don't know how we all made it, all of us living with just my grandmother . . . *my dad, he was in jail.*

Chad: I needed someone to help me through all the changes and problems . . . when I was growing up . . . *I didn't have a dad*, never knew the motherfucker.*

Will: The apartment complex we lived in . . . just my grandma and me and two of my cousins . . . it was a rough place . . . we all had to stick together . . . my mom died when I was young and *my dad, fuck man, I don't even know where that son of a bitch is.*

Nate: Without my ma . . . you see, she made sure we at least had the necessities . . . she was our support . . . she taught us the difference between right and wrong . . . but *it was still real hard not having a father around.*

Socioeconomic Status

Lawrence: We were so goddamn *poor* . . . and the apartments we lived in, my Mom, and me and my three sisters . . . it was terrible.*

Alan: There were times, times we *didn't have enough money* to buy things like milk. . . .

Abe: We lived in the *poorest part of town* . . . the south side, let me tell you, it's rough on a young man growing up in those conditions.

Jimmy: Son, we was dirt fucking *poor*.

Lenny: I don't know how the hell we survived looking back, man . . . it was hard . . . especially since dad took off on mom just after I was born . . . I know it was *financially very hard* for mom.*

Urban/Rural Location

Shawn: I was raised up in a rough section of *Detroit* and let me tell you . . . all of us boys, well, it wasn't a place I'd want to raise my kids.*

Adam: I grew up in *Birmingham* . . . we ran the fucking streets there, and got into a lot of shit we shouldn't have.*

Dave: I lived with one of my aunts in *Chicago* . . . my childhood, man, was all fucked up, I saw my brother get shot right in front of our apartment, I ain't never got over that shit.*

Eric: Well, I was born in Los Angeles and lived there most of my life . . . we left when my uncle sent me to a private school in *Kentucky* . . . let me say, leaving that slum that I spent my childhood in probably saved me.

Bobby: I was raised by my mother and father on a farm in *Kansas* . . . I would say I had a pretty traditional childhood.

Jeff: I grew up in a rural part of *Tennessee* . . . I can't complain, I had everything I needed, my parents were pretty good to me.

Childhood Friends

Alex: My neighborhood, man, that place was fucked up . . . I saw five good *friends get gunned down* in broad daylight, and for what, it was just a fucked up place.*

Jake: I had *friends, too many to count, they didn't make it* [were killed before the completion of high school].

Chris: A lot of people I know . . . almost *everybody I know from my neighborhood has been shot* or stabbed at least once.*

Derek: I had some good friends that I hung with . . . but, now, *they weren't real friends* . . . actually, I feel sorry for them now . . . the ones that's still alive.

Jamal: *I had my boys* . . . we was pretty fucking tight . . . man *we got into some shit* though . . . I probably wouldn't have been as fucked up, but I was basically raised in a group home . . . my mom was all fucked up on crack and I ain't got no fucking dad.*

The qualitative findings from this theme were some the most important. Overall, the data revealed two constants for these players: (1) they all experienced "sudden" newfound affluence and fame, and (2) most were involved in an assortment of deviant behaviors, some illegal. My argument then is that many experienced anomie and engaged in deviant behavior because, first, they encountered a sudden change in wealth and status, and second, because they did *not* have adequate social ties and support. In fact, it appears that a majority of players who were anomic and deviant appeared to not have access to adequate forms of social support.

Ideal-Typical Social Ties/Support (And Lack Thereof)

During a conversation over lunch at an NFL training camp, Randy, whom I had met earlier that year, told me that he wanted to introduce me to a player that had been involved in a series of deviant and illegal activities. Randy was one of the few *very* "well adjusted" and "grounded" players that was part of this study group. He was, as one of his teammates described him, "just a good guy." Randy was aware of my research (through Soloman) and thought that one of his teammates, Wesley, would be willing to speak with me. At that time, Randy had been volunteering his services as a mentor to Wesley, trying to help him get his life and priorities back in order.

After some small talk, Randy assured Wesley that I was okay and that what he told me would be kept confidential. I further verified to Wesley that our conversation would not end up a headline in the following morning's newspaper. At that point, he began to explain how his lack of social support (especially family) had contributed to his unhappiness with life, and how his unhappiness had contributed to his deviance.

I asked him what his experience had been thus far in the NFL and if playing professional football had been what he had always wanted to do. He responded, "I guess it was something I always wanted to do, but why do guys want to play in the NFL? The money, the fame, the women, the jewelry, the cars, the houses." He continued, "The problem is, there's only so many cars you can buy. There are only so many women you can sleep with. There's only so much all your money can buy. I mean really." He went on to tell me that he had acquired everything he had ever wanted, yet as he revealed, "I still wasn't happy."

He commented further, "A lot of players like to tell people and themselves that football isn't their life . . . and, when I talk about football, I'm not just talking about playing the game, I'm talking about the lifestyle, livin' fast, being reckless." He added, "Well they lying, that's not true. . . . To a lot of guys, it's their life, it's everything. I realized it was my life. It shouldn't be your life but somehow it is." At this point, he started talking about the importance of having a social support network. As he explained, "you got to have some other interest, family, a wife, kids, even a good friend, something to turn to when things ain't working out on the field, and especially, when the temptations come knocking at your door. I didn't have any of that, I didn't have those kinds of interests." He continued, "When you allow yourself to get caught up in the lifestyle, and you ain't got no family, no nothing to go home to, nobody to say, hey, you better check yourself, you're in trouble. . . . That was me, I got caught, I really got caught."

Later that afternoon, Randy told me more about Wesley's background. Wesley grew up in an urban ghetto and was raised by his mom. He never knew his father and his two brothers were killed during a drive-by shooting when he was a young boy. Two weeks into college, he was informed that his mom had died from cancer. So when he was drafted into the NFL, he did not have any "close" family to turn to for support. And, it appeared to me that the lack of social support he received from his family was a contributing factor to his personal anomie and deviance.

Regrettably, this story was representative of many of the players I interviewed. Players' lack of social ties/support combined with instant wealth and fame appeared to produce anomic characteristics, which, in turn, created an environment conducive to deviance. However, when social support was present, it did appear to buffer the often negative effects of anomie.

The opposite of Wesley, Randy was a veteran player in the league. He was the guy that most of the young players turned to for advice. And, from my observations, everybody appeared to genuinely like him (something that was rare). His background was very traditional in nature. He was raised in a small town by both parents. His family was a tight knit group, according to him. They were very religious, and Randy is too. He is married and credits his wife "with keeping [him] in line."

During my first interview with him, he told me what many others had said before, that the transition from college to the NFL was a very difficult one. He commented that, "Being recognized [famous] everywhere you go, dealing with the pressures of playing pro football, and dealing with the many temptations you face daily is extremely difficult." But he went on to say, "When I get myself into a bind, and I'm not perfect, I rely on my family. . . . They are always there for me, they don't judge me, they are very supportive."

Randy was one of the few in the study group who had a lot of social support, who was integrated into a social group such as family, and who was regulated by various institutions such as marriage and religion. This kind of support made it possible for him to cope with the life change associated with entry into the NFL. Players like Randy appeared to be better able to avoid getting caught up in the "NFL lifestyle." They appeared to be happier, less anomic, and less likely to engage in destructive and deviant behaviors.

Notes

1. An asterisk indicates that the player from whom the quote came was arrested after entering the NFL.

2. It should be noted that there was a latent presence of themes surrounding institutional discrimination (racism) in the interview data. Many of the African-American players who participated in this study talked about being marginalized and set up for failure (e.g., in our education and economic system). They felt they had to rely on their athletic prowess to achieve success. These issues concerning race are extremely important for the discussion of professional athletes in American culture. However, this is not the primary focus of this particular book. For an excellent discussion on race and professional athletes, see William C. Rhoden, *Forty Million Dollar Slaves: The Rise, Fall, and Redemption of the Black Athlete* (New York: Three Rivers Press, 2007).

Chapter Seven

Moving the Chains: From Observation to Quantification

Qualitative Research Questions and Generalized Observations

The elite interviews I conducted with the two key informants, and the in-depth interviews with other players raised the following questions: First, why are so many NFL players involved in deviant and/or illegal activities? Second, given the consistent qualitative findings about being unhappy and unable to cope with wealth and change, does anomie (an attitudinal attribute) contribute to the deviant behavior? Third, does the presence of social ties such as family structure, early socialization experiences, level of education, presence of religious belief, and a network of friends act as a buffer against anomie and deviant behavior? These questions were central to the objectives of the study I conducted for this book. The questions express the "core" themes from the athletes interviewed and observed.

As a result of the field work, which has included hours of interviews with the two key informants and 104 interviews with current and former NFL players, the following generalized observations can be made. Within the study group, a substantial number of players had prior experience with deviant and illegal behaviors and activities. Many reported problems with coping upon entering the NFL and sought to find personal fulfillment and happiness despite wealth and popular recognition. I think this indicates that some level of anomie is present in a number of these players' lives. Yet many other players reported being satisfied and appear to have adjusted to the pressures of the NFL. Social ties appeared to play a key role in the level of happiness and overall life satisfaction for these players. In many of the interviews, players spoke about relationships that gave meaning to life. For many players who are dissatisfied with life in the NFL, social support structures appeared to be absent.

Quantitative Variables and Hypotheses

After a review of (1) the current literature (Benedict 1997; Benedict & Yaeger 1998; Blumstein & Benedict 1999) which documents the growing concern over the deviant and illegal acts among many NFL players, (2) Durkheim's classic work ([1897] 1951) that posits the concept of anomie as a social reality, and (3) the qualitative findings from the field research, several social psychological, attitudinal themes emerged.

Law-Abiding versus Law-Breaking Players

A number of players in the study group described themselves as having been arrested and broken the law since joining the NFL, but others did not. What are the correlates for players, in the study group, who abide by the law versus those who do not? Because some players have been involved in law-breaking behavior, it seems plausible to hypothesize that these players possess higher levels of anomie.

Anomie

Durkheim ([1897] 1951) and others have suggested that anomie is a social psychological attribute (Srole 1956). If anomie can be found to be higher in some NFL players, it is reasonable to hypothesize that players who possess higher levels of anomie have identifiable correlates that are different from the correlates of NFL players who possess lower to non-measurable levels of anomie.

Happy with Life versus Unhappy with Life

A number of players described themselves as being unhappy. During the interviews, several told me they were searching for ways to become happy. If anomie is defined as a state of meaninglessness and life without a sense of regulation or control (Durkheim [1897] 1951; Kornhauser 1978), it is plausible to hypothesize that the level of happiness is associated with anomie and select other correlates that relate to the players' level of happiness. I would hypothesize that higher levels of anomie are correlated with higher levels of unhappiness. Moreover, higher levels of unhappiness should be associated more strongly with law-breaking players as compared to players who have not broken the law.

Wealth and Aspiration

One clearly articulated theme during the field work was the sense of personal aspiration and the desire to be wealthy by the players in the study group. This desire for money and success indicates a tremendous change in lifestyle for most players. Given the sense of desire for wealth and desire to aspire, I would hypothesize that the stronger the levels of wealth and aspiration present in these players, the higher the possibility of the presence of anomie.

Social Ties/Support

In the qualitative data, players spoke of their need for relationships that provide stability and meaning. These relationships ranged from discussion about relationships with God, to marriage, and to life in school. It would appear these relationships provide a sense of social ties and support. Thus, it is reasonable to hypothesize that players who feel less supported through relationships possess higher levels of anomie. These players seem more likely to be unhappy and to be law breakers.

Early Socialization

Players often spoke about where they came from and the impact of family on their lives. I would hypothesize that players who possess a stronger sense of family support, and come from low-crime cities and neighborhoods, should possess lower levels of anomie, be happier, not be involved in law-breaking activities, and possess a more moderate view about what it takes to be successful in life.

Hypotheses Synthesized

Life in the NFL, as experienced by the athletes in the study group, changed their personal and professional lives. Many players described themselves as participating in deviant behaviors. A number of players admitted they had been arrested and broken the law. The players spoke often of being happy or unhappy with their new life in the NFL. Players spoke often of the desire for wealth and fame, yet many admitted it came at a cost to their personal lives. A sense of meaningful social ties/support played a role for many players. Many players referred to lingering childhood memories. Hence, relationships and early socialization experiences likely played some role in players' ability to adapt to the fast-paced life of the NFL. Each of these factors may well have contributed in some manner to whether a player possesses some identifiable level of anomie. The presence and level of anomie may be an important factor in describing whether a player living within the law is happy or unhappy with life, and feels he has an adequate or an inadequate social support system. It also may correspond with how they relate to others due, in part, to the influence of early socialization factors, and to their sheer desire to achieve wealth and success.

Quantitative Methods

The use of quantitative methods evolved as a result of the elite and specialized interviews with the two key informants. During the course of those interviews it became apparent that a systematic gathering of data could be achieved through a structured interview guide/questionnaire. The qualitative data gathered during the field work allowed for open-ended interviews that provided a breadth and, at times, a depth to the data. A potential problem with this method of data collection can be the lack of comparability within the study group. Therefore, the structured interview guide/questionnaire allowed for response to common questions and statements. The use of statistics for descriptive purposes also allowed for additional description and understanding of the data.

The Study Situation

Quantitative data to assess anomie and deviance among 104 current and former NFL players were collected from 2001 to 2006. The athletes were located in Ohio, Kentucky, Kansas, Missouri, Texas, and Florida. The study conducted for this book is the result of elite and specialized interviews with two key informants, both former NFL players. The two key informants frequently expressed a desire to assess the outbreak of deviant acts committed by NFL players.

Sample Selection

In 2001, data collection was initiated using a non-probability sampling technique—a snowball sample (Berg 2001). Snowball samples are particularly useful in studying deviance, sensitive topics, and hard-to-reach populations such as professional athletes. The key "strategy of snowballing involves first identifying several people with relevant characteristics and interviewing [or surveying] them. . . . These subjects are then asked for the names of other people who possess the same attributes they do" (Berg 2001: 33). For this book, the key informants helped secure entrée to the players in the study group.

Random or other probability formats were not possible due to the difficult nature of entrance into this group. Contacts were made through an intricate network of friendships of the two informants. Once a player agreed to participate in the study, a questionnaire was either self-administered or administered by me. I collected data via 73 self-administered questionnaires and 31 phone interviews. The athletes were provided ample opportunity to ask questions and make additional comments about the questionnaires, and their oral responses were recorded.

Instrument Construction

A structured questionnaire was used for data collection. The questionnaire was explained to the player in detail and then administered. If the athlete seemed hesitant or did not quite understand how to complete the questionnaire, I carefully explained the answering procedures. The research techniques used to gather data included socio-demographic, attitudinal, and deviance-oriented data about the player, and Likert-type scales and indices designed to measure anomie, wealth/aspiration, social ties/support, and early socialization.

Confidentiality, anonymity, and informed consent had high priority in the research I conducted for this book. Explanation was given that the research was focused on group attributes rather than individuals' responses to the questionnaire. This explanation helped the athletes feel more at ease during the process of data collection. The research procedures were guided by the code of ethics of the American Sociological Association (ASA). Each player was notified, both orally and on the questionnaire/interview guide, of his rights as a subject. No names were used at any point during the study. All completed questionnaires/interview guides and interviews are coded by numbers to ensure anonymity.

Characteristics of the Sample

The sample was composed of 45 (43%) current NFL players and 59 (57%) former or retired players. The mean age of the respondents was 30.10, ranging from 22 to 39. There were 40 (38.5%) Caucasian respondents and 64 (61.5%) African-American respondents. The range for years played in the NFL was from 1 to 11, with 4.52 being the average. There were 50 (48.1%) players who reported being married and 54 (51.9%) not married; 37 (35.6%) reported being college graduates while 67 (64.4%) were not; 69 (66.3%) reported having a relationship with God/higher power while 35 (33.7%) did not; 41 (39.4%) reported earning $500,000 or less per year and 63 (60.6%) earned more than $500,000.

In reviewing early socialization variables, 38 (36.5%) reported being raised in a two parent/guardian household and 66 (63.5%) said they were raised in a single parent/guardian household; 39 (37.5%) reported growing up in a rural location while 65 (62.5%) grew up in an urban location; and 42 (40.4%) reported being raised in a middle class or above family or household, while 62 (59.6%) said they were raised in a lower class or poor family or household.

When asked about their current life situation, 58 (55.8%) reported being happy and 46 (44.2%) unhappy; 26 (25%) reported having received some sort of counseling or rehabilitation, while 78 (75%) said they had not received counseling/rehabilitation; and 71 (68.3%) reported being law abiders (after entrance into the NFL), while 33 (31.7%) reported breaking the law. (The summary of the sample data is presented in Table 1).

Operationalization of Dependent Variables

After identifying the themes in the qualitative findings and the application of anomie theory, three dependent variables were operationalized. First, in order to operationalize deviance, players were asked whether they have been involved in law-breaking or law-abiding behavior. Second, the theoretical construct of anomie was treated as a social psychological attribute and operationalized as a ten-item scale. For the third, players reported either being happy or unhappy with life. This third variable was frequently mentioned during the qualitative interviews. It was included as a dependent variable because it represents behavioral characteristics that helped to describe how these players felt about their life situation and was theoretically related to the presence or absence of anomie.

Table 1: Summary Descriptive Statistics for the Study Group (N = 104)

Characteristic		Sample Data	Frequency
Age:	Mean	30.10	
	Standard Deviation	4.028	
	Range	22 to 39	
Race:	Percent White	38.5%	40
	Percent Black	61.5%	64
Player Status:	Percent Current	42.3%	45
	Percent Former/Retired	56.7%	59
Years played in the NFL:	Mean	4.52	
	Standard Deviation	2.014	
	Range	1 to 11	
Marital Status:	Percent Married	48.1%	50
	Percent Not Married	51.9%	54
Education:	Percent Graduated College	35.6%	37
	Percent Not Graduated College	64.4%	67
Income (After entering the NFL):	Percent Earning $0-$500,00	39.4%	41
	Percent Earning $500,001 and above	60.6%	63
Family Structure:	Percent Raised in Two Parent/Guardian Home	36.5%	38
	Percent Raised in Single Parent/Guardian Home	63.5%	66
Location (First ten years of life):	Percent Raised in Rural Location	37.5%	39
	Percent Raised in Urban Location	62.5%	65

Table 1 Continued: Summary Descriptive Statistics for the Study Group (N = 104)

Characteristic		Sample Data	Frequency
Social Class (Self reported):	Percent Raised Middle Class and Above	40.4%	42
	Percent Raised Lower Class/Poor	59.6%	62
Religion:	Percent that has Relationship with God/higher Power	66.3%	69
	Percent that does not have Relationship with God/higher Power	33.7%	35
Level of Happiness:	Percent Happy	55.8%	58
	Percent Unhappy	44.2%	46
Counseling/Rehabilitation:	Percent Receiving Counseling/Rehabilitation	25.0%	26
	Percent Not Receiving Counseling/Rehabilitation	75.0%	78
Criminal Activity:	Percent Law Abiders	68.3%	71
	Percent Law Breakers	31.7%	33

Law Abiders versus Law Breakers

In Table 1, law abiders versus law breakers was operationalized as a dichotomous variable. It should be noted that "law abiders" referred to those who had not been arrested after joining the NFL and that "law breakers" referred to those who had been arrested after entering the NFL. The responses were weighted 0 for "law abiders" and 1 for "law breakers." Approximately, one-third of the athletes were self-reported law breakers with 33 players (31.7%) being law breakers and 71 players (68.3 %) being law abiders. The literature on NFL players (Benedict & Yaeger 1998) suggested that approximately 20 percent were law breakers. This study group had a rate of law breakers higher than other sampled groups.

Anomie

The theoretical construct of anomie was operationalized as a ten-item Likert-type scale. See Table 2 for the anomie scale. Items were coded 3 to 0, with a weight of 3 representing "strongly agree," 2 representing "agree," 1 "disagree," and 0 "strongly disagree." The scores of the ten items were summed and divided by ten to create a scale ranging from a low of 0, meaning low anomie, to a high of 3, meaning high anomie.

The first five items were from Srole's (1956) anomia scale. The anomia scale has been widely used over the past fifty years and has been regarded by many as a reliable measure for assessing rapid change, malintegration, and meaninglessness in the lives of individuals (Clinard 1964; Orru 1987). The Srole scale was intended to measure the concepts of meaninglessness, unhappiness, and the degree the individual is integrated into a social group.

Orru (1987) believed that "anomia expresses the malintegration or dysfunctional relation of individuals to their social worlds" (126). In other words, the individual with anomic characteristics will tend to be disconnected from (1) the larger political norms of society, (2) the larger cultural norms of society, (3) the larger economic norms of society, (4) "internalized social norms and values," and (5) the main socialization group (Srole 1956: 711).

The sixth item in the anomie scale is from the Neal and Seeman (1964) powerlessness scale. This item was included because it measures a sense of helplessness that is theoretically similar to aspects of Srole's (1956) conceptualization of anomia.

Table 2: Ten-Item Attitude Anomie Scale and Weighting Values for Each Item (N=104)

Statement	Possible Responses			
Weighting Value	Strongly Agree	Agree	Disagree	Strongly Disagree
1. In spite of what people say, the lot of the average man is getting worse.	3	2	1	0
2. It's hardly fair to bring children into the world with the way things look for the future.	3	2	1	0
3. Nowadays a person has to live pretty much for today and let tomorrow take care of itself.	3	2	1	0
4. These days a person doesn't know who he can count on.	3	2	1	0
5. There's little use writing to public officials because they aren't really interested in the problems of the average man.	3	2	1	0
6. More and more I feel helpless in the face of what's happening in the world today.	3	2	1	0
7. There is too much drinking of alcoholic beverages today.	3	2	1	0
8. People should never smoke marijuana because it leads to a life of drugs.	3	2	1	0
9. Almost everyone finds leisure time more satisfying than work.	3	2	1	0
10. Today's sexual morality seems to be, "anything goes."	3	2	1	0

Items 1-5: Srole (1956)
Item 6: Neal and Seeman (1964)
Items 7-10: Abrahamson (1980)

Other Neal and Seeman items were originally included, but were dropped due to theoretical and statistical incompatibility with anomia items.

The remaining four items were from the Abrahamson (1980) gratification scale. These items focus on approval or disapproval of contemporary patterns of indulgence and pleasure such as consumption of alcohol, drug use, leisure time, and sexual standards/values. These items center on the degree to which people accept or condemn "what they perceive as the styles that are in vogue" (Abrahamson 1980: 52). Theoretically, these items should be closely associated with behaviors that accompany malintegration, meaninglessness, and powerlessness.

Happy versus Unhappy with Life

In Table 1, the degree of player happiness was reported and operationalized as a dichotomous variable. The responses were weighted 0 for "unhappy" players and 1 for "happy" players. Forty-six players (44.2%)—nearly one-half of the study group—self-reported being unhappy with life. Fifty-eight players (55.8%) reported being happy. A recent Gallup poll (Saad 2004) found that 4% of Americans were unhappy with their current life situation. Approximately 95% reported being happy. This contrasts sharply with the NFL players who composed the study group.

Operationalization of Independent Variables

The variables selected as independent variables in the study were (1) wealth/aspiration, (2) social ties/support, (3) early socialization, (4) rehabilitation/counseling, (5) income after entering the NFL, (6) age, (7) race, and (8) years played in the NFL. These variables were selected because of their representation of theoretical concepts often associated with anomie and deviance. These variables were frequently cited in many of the qualitative interviews.

Wealth/Aspiration

Wealth/Aspiration was operationalized as a three-item Likert-type index. See Table 3 for the wealth/attainment index. The index was constructed by assigning scores of 0, 1, 2, and 3 to "strongly disagree," "disagree," "agree," and "strongly disagree," respectively, in answer to each question. The scores of the three items were then summed and divided by three to create an index ranging from 0 to 3.

These three items were originally constructed and included in the Abrahamson (1980) attainment scale. This index focused on an individual's desire to aspire and become wealthy. Moreover, these items centered on people's commitment to strive for wealth and attainments and their perceptions of enjoying wealth and prosperity. In essence, this index emphasized wealth and attainment orientations.

Social Ties/Support

Social ties/support was operationalized as a three-item index. See Table 4 for the social ties/support index. The index was constructed by assigning scores of 0 and 1 to "no" and "yes," respectively, in answer to each question. The scores of the three items were then summed and divided by three to create an index ranging from 0 to 1.

This index focused on social ties and support systems of marriage, education, and religiosity, all of which appear to have buffering qualities against anomie and deviance. From the qualitative data, the relationships gained and maintained through marriage, education, and religiosity appeared to indicate the importance of social ties and support.

Table 3: Three-Item Attitude Index for Wealth-Aspiration and Weighting for Each Item (N=104)

Statement	Possible Responses			
	Strongly Disagree	Agree	Disagree	Strongly Disagree
Weighting Value	0	2	1	0
1. It is not natural for people to try hard to become wealthy.	0	2	1	0
2. It is natural for people to enjoy being wealthy.	0	2	1	0
3. I admire people who try to be the best at whatever they do.	0	2	1	0

Items 1-3: Abrahamson (1980)

Table 4: Three-Item Attitude Index for Social Ties/Support and Weighting for Each Item (N=104)

Statement	Possible Responses	
	Yes	No
Weighting Value	1	0
1. I have a personal relationship with God/Higher Power.	1	0
2. I am married.	1	0
3. I have graduated from college	1	0

Early Socialization

Early socialization was operationalized as a two-item index. See Table 5 for the early socialization index. The index was constructed by assigning scores of 0 and 1 to, first, "two parent/guardian household" and "single parent/guardian household," respectively, and second, 0 and 1 to "rural" and "urban," respectively, to answers given to each question. The scores of the two items were then summed and divided by two to create an index ranging from 0 to 1. The qualitative data indicated that family structure and geographic location were both important factors in one's early socialization process.

Counseling/Rehabilitation

Counseling/rehabilitation was operationalized as a dichotomous variable. The responses were weighted 0 for "no" and 1 for "yes." (see Table 1).

Income (after entering the NFL)

Income was operationalized as a dichotomous variable. The responses were weighted 0 for "$0-$500,000" and 1 for "$500,001 and above." (see Table 1).

Table 5: Two-Item Attitude Index for Early Socialization and Weighting for Each Item (N=104)

Statement	Possible Responses	
Weighting Value	1	0
1. I was raised by one or two parents.	Single Parent 1	Two Parents 0
2. How would you describe where you lived for the first ten years of your life?	Urban 1	Rural 0

Age

Age was operationalized as age of the respondent at last birthdate. (see Table 1).

Race

Race was operationalized as a dichotomous variable. The responses were weighted 0 for "White" and 1 for "Black." (see Table 1).

Years Played in the NFL

Years played in the NFL was operationalized by asking the respondent how many years he had played in the NFL. (see Table 1).

Reliability Analysis of the Scales/Indices

In order to construct composite measures of anomie, wealth/attainment, social ties/support, and early socialization a considerable number of items presumably relating to each attribute were subjected to a range of factor analyses, bivariate correlational analyses, and reliability analyses. Those items that exceedingly overlapped the four dimensions were systematically taken out until items relating to the four constructs were finally distinguishable from each other. The items and their loadings are presented in Tables 6, 7, 8, and 9 respectively.

In conjunction with factor analysis, the reliability of the anomie scale and the wealth/aspiration, social ties/support, and early socialization in-

Table 6: Correlation Matrix*, Standardized Item Alpha Reliability Coefficient**, and Factor Analysis for Anomie Scale (N=104)

	Item 1	Item 2	Item 3	Item 4	Item 5	Item 6	Item 7	Item 8	Item 9	Item 10	Factor Loading
Item 1	1.00										0.626
Item 2	0.707	1.00									0.541
Item 3	0.693	0.611	1.00								0.732
Item 4	0.687	0.540	0.572	1.00							0.591
Item 5	0.612	0.580	0.423	0.539	1.00						0.520
Item 6	0.604	0.548	0.485	0.486	0.455	1.00					0.420
Item 7	0.688	0.619	0.656	0.690	0.548	0.543	1.00				0.702
Item 8	0.729	0.673	0.671	0.696	0.589	0.594	0.901	1.00			0.731
Item 9	0.625	0.536	0.661	0.512	0.523	0.480	0.616	0.625	1.00		0.738
Item 10	0.485	0.484	0.591	0.543	0.354	0.404	0.546	0.577	0.519	1.00	0.709

Standardized Item Alpha Reliability Coefficient = 0.933

Eigenvalue = 11.16
Percent of Variance = 41.7

*All Correlations are significant at the 0.001 level.
**Standardized Item Alpha is computed as: alpha = $kr/1+(k-1)\bar{r}$ where k equals the number of items in the scale and $\bar{r}$ equals the average correlation between items.

Table 7: Correlation Matrix*, Standardized Item Reliability Coefficient**, and Factor Analysis for Wealth/Aspiration Index (N=104)

	Item 1	Item 2	Item 3	Factor Loading
Item 1	1.00			0.597
Item 2	0.511	1.00		0.719
Item 3	0.323	0.590	1.00	0.750
Standardized Item Alpha Reliability Coefficient = 0.731				Eigenvalue = 1.78 Percent of Variance = 50.6

* All correlations are significant at the 0.01 level.
** Standardized Item Alpha is computed as: alpha = $k\bar{r}/1+(k-1)\bar{r}$; where k equals the number of items in the index and $\bar{r}$ equals the average correlation between items.

Table 8: Correlation Matrix*, Standardized Item Reliability Coefficient**, and Factor Analysis for Social Ties/Support Index (N=104)

	Item 1	Item 2	Item 3	Factor Loading
Item 1	1.00			0.609
Item 2	0.531	1.00		0.392
Item 3	0.400	0.444	1.00	0.341
Standardized Item Alpha Reliability Coefficient = 0.718				Eigenvalue = 1.15 Percent of Variance = 60.1

*All correlations are significant at the 0.01 level.
**Standardized Item Alpha is computed as: alpha = $k\bar{r}/1+(k-1)\bar{r}$; where k equals the number of items in the index and $\bar{r}$ equals the average correlation between items.

Table 9: Correlation Matrix*, Standardized Item Reliability Coefficient**, and Factor Analysis for Early Socialization Index (N=104)

	Item 1	Item 2	Item 3	Factor Loading
Item 1	1.00			0.609
Item 2	0.567	1.00		0.392
Standardized Item Alpha Reliability Coefficient = 0.724				Eigenvalue = 1.75 Percent of Variance = 47.8

*All correlations are significant at the 0.01 level.
**Standardized Item Alpha is computed as: alpha = $k\bar{r}/1+(k-1)\bar{r}$; where k equals the number of items in the index and $\bar{r}$ equals the average correlation between items.

dices were evaluated using the standardized item alpha. The standardized item alpha measured the total scale reliability of multi-item additive scales/indices. The purpose of the reliability measure was to check the internal consistency of the measurement instrument. Scale/Index reliability was measured between 0.0 and 1.0 as a positive value. The higher the value, the greater the reliability of the measurement instrument.

The standardized item alpha for the anomie scale and three indices are as follows: anomie (0.9332), wealth/aspiration (0.7309), social ties/support (0.7175), and early socialization (0.7238). The intercorrelations among the scale/indices' items are presented in Tables 6, 7, 8, and 9 respectively. Although the three indices had somewhat lower levels of multicolinearity than the anomie scale, a reliability coefficient of over 0.7 is still relatively high for social science research (Nunnally 1978). Since the reliability coefficients for the anomie scale and the three indices were relatively high, I concluded that composite indices could be developed for the four variables.

Statistical Analyses

Multiple correlation, discriminant analysis, logistic regression, and stepwise regression analyses were used to assess relationships among the study variables. Each of these parametric statistical analyses was used because of the robust nature and strength of each statistic. The more robust statistical analysis, hence, provided a more comprehensive description of the study group being examined (Nunnally 1978).

In order to use parametric analyses, the assumption was made that Likert-type scale/index scores met the requirements of ordered-metric measures (Labovitz 1967, 1970; Ableson & Tukey 1970). According to Labovitz (1970), "Empirical evidence supports the treatment of ordinal variables *as if* they conform to interval scales. Although some small error may accompany the treatment of ordinal variables as interval, this is offset by the use of more powerful, more sensitive, better developed, and more clearly interpretable statistics with known sampling error" (515). In essence, it has been demonstrated that ordered-metric scales can be meaningfully analyzed by the use of parametric statistics.

Multiple correlation was used to test the hypotheses and to determine the direction of the relationships between independent variables and the three dependent variables. Discriminant analyses were used in order to distinguish between two or more groups of cases. The objective of this type of analysis was to weight and linearly combine the discriminating variables in such a way that the groups are forced to be statistically distinct. In essence, the goal of discriminant analysis was "to be able to 'discriminate' between the groups in the sense of being able to tell them apart" (Klecka 1975: 435). It should be noted that, theoretically, the assumption of discriminant analysis is that the discriminating variables have a multivariate normal distribution and equal variance-covariance matrices within each group. However, according to Klecka (1975), since, in practice, the technique is very robust, these assumptions need not be strongly adhered to (435).

Logistic regression analysis was used to verify the findings of each discriminant analysis. Logistic regression is especially appropriate when the dependent variable is dichotomous in nature (Morgan & Teachman 1988). In assessing the covariates of law abiders versus law breakers and in assessing the covariates of happy versus unhappy, logistic regression was an appropriate statistic when interpreted along with the findings from discriminant analysis (Press & Wilson 1978).

Multiple regression analysis was utilized in examining the covariates of the anomie scale. In addition, multiple regression analysis was performed to determine the relative explanatory power of the independent variables when all variables were considered at the same time. In essence, multiple regression allows more than one independent variable to have an influence on the dependent variable (George & Mallery 2003).

Thus for the quantitative portion of the study that was conducted for this book, I chose to use multiple correlation, discriminant, logistic regression, and multiple regression statistics in order to examine the relationships among the variables of law abiders versus law breakers, anomie, happy versus unhappy with life, wealth/aspiration, social ties/support, early socialization, rehabilitation/counseling, income after entering the NFL, age, race, and years played in the NFL.

References

Abelson, Robert. P., and John. W. Tukey. 1970. Efficient conversion of non-metric information into metric information. In *The quantitative analysis of social problems*, ed. E. R. Tufte, 407-417. Reading, MA: Addison Wesley.

Abrahamson, Mark. 1980. Sudden wealth, gratification and attainment: Durkheim's anomie of affluence reconsidered. *American Sociological Review* 45: 49-57.

Benedict, Jeff. 1997. *Public heroes, private felons*. Boston: Northeastern University Press.

Benedict, Jeff, and Don Yaeger. 1998. *Pros and cons: The criminals who play in the NFL*. New York: Warner Books.

Berg, Bruce L. 2001. *Qualitative research methods for the social sciences*. Boston: Allyn and Bacon.

Blumstein, Alfred, and Jeff Benedict. 1999. Criminal violence of NFL players compared to the general population. *Chance* 12: 12-15.

Clinard, Marshall B., ed. 1964. *Anomie and deviant behavior*. New York: Free Press.

Durkheim, Emile. [1897] 1951. *Suicide*. Trans. John A. Spaulding and George Simpson. New York: Free Press.

George, Darren, and Paul Mallery. 2003. *SPSS for Windows*. Boston: Allyn and Bacon.

Klecka, William R. 1975. Discriminant analysis. In *SPSS: Statistical package for the social sciences*, 2nd ed. Eds. Norman Nie, Hadlai Hull, Jean Jenkins, Karin Steinbrenner, and Dale Bent, 434-467. New York: McGraw Hill.

Kornhauser, Ruth R. 1978. *Social sources of delinquency: An appraisal of analytic models*. Chicago: University of Chicago Press.

Labovitz, Sanford. 1967. Some observations on measurement and statistics. *Social Forces* 46: 151-160.

———. 1970. The assignment of numbers to rank order categories. *American Sociological Review* 35: 515-524.

Morgan, Philip S., and Jay D. Teachman. 1988. Logistic regression: Description, examples, and comparisons. *Journal of Marriage and the Family* 50: 929-936.

Neal, Arthur G., and Melvin Seeman. 1964. Organizations and powerlessness. *American Sociological Review* 29: 216-226.

Nunnally, Jum C. 1978. *Psychometric theory*. New York: McGraw Hill.

Orru, Marco. 1987. *Anomie: History and meanings*. Boston: George Allen & Unwin.

Press, James S., and Sandra Wilson. 1978. Choosing between logistic regression and discriminant analysis. *Journal of the American Statistical Association* 73: 699-705.

Saad, Lydia. 2004. A nation of happy people. *Gallup News Service*, http://www.freepublic.com/focus/f-news/1051689/posts > (accessed July 6, 2006).

Srole, Leo. 1956. Social integration and certain corollaries: An exploratory study. *American Sociological Review* 21: 709-716.

Chapter Eight

The Final Score: What the Numbers Mean

Before being subjected to multivariate analyses, the data were examined using descriptive statistics. I calculated descriptive statistics in order to examine the central tendencies, frequency, and range patterns within the variables. Descriptive data for the attitude scales/indices are presented followed by the correlation, discriminant, logistic regression, and multiple regression analyses.

Response to the Attitude Items

The descriptive data for the anomie scale are presented in Table 1. The data basically reveal that many of the players held slightly anomic perceptions (perceptions that would appear to represent anomic characteristics and behaviors for this study group) toward life. Anomie scores are interpreted as follows: (a) scores of 0-1.59 represent a low level of anomie, (b) scores of 1.6-1.99 represent a moderate level of anomie, and (c) scores of 2.00-3.00 represent a high level of anomie.

On the first item, the mean score was 1.58 which indicated that on average a low to moderate level of players perceived the situation of the average person as getting worse not better. The second item had a mean of 1.53 revealing that on average a low to moderate level of players perceived the future to be bleak. The third item had a mean of 1.83, which revealed that, on average, a moderate level of athletes' perceptions were of "living for today." The fourth item also had a mean of 1.83, which indicated that on average a moderate level of players perceived that people do not have anyone they can count on. The fifth item had a mean of 1.74 which represented that a moderate level of players perceived that public officials are not interested in the problems of the average person. The sixth item had a mean score of 1.39, which indicated that on average players reported a low level of feeling helpless. The seventh item had a mean score of 1.54, which indicated that on average a moderate level of athletes in the study group perceived that people drink too much alcohol. The eighth item had a mean score of 1.33, which indicated that on average a low level of players perceived that people should not smoke marijuana. The ninth item had a mean score of 1.81, which revealed that on average a moderate level of players perceived that people typically enjoy leisure time more than work. And lastly, the tenth item had a mean score of 2.48, which indicated that on average a high level of NFL players in the study group perceived today's sexual morality as "anything goes."

The majority of items demonstrated that many of the NFL players in the study group held some degree of anomic perceptions, as six of the ten items fell in the moderate to high range of anomie, and two other items fell in the low/moderate range. The highest mean score that stands out, which is supported by the qualitative data, is the perception that traditional sexual behavior or morality is a thing of the past. Of the athletes, 90 of 104 agreed that sexual morality nowadays appears to be "anything goes." Promiscuous or alternative sexual behavior appeared to be the norm for a high number of players. There were three other items that revealed relatively high mean scores: Items 3, 4, and 9. Item three may represent the anomic characteristic of instant gratification and not worrying about the future consequences of one's actions, as this was a consistent qualitative finding as well. Item four potentially indicated another anomic characteristic and qualitative finding: that during times of change "quality" relationships are important but, for many in this study group, rare. And item nine appeared to reveal that many of the athletes found leisure time more important than work. This possibly helps to explain the mean score of item eight (the drug use item), as over half of the players reported that they disagreed that people should never smoke marijuana. This conclusion is drawn in conjunction with the qualitative findings that revealed that a number of players in the study group reported drug use as a leisure activity, an activity that is typically viewed as outside of normative bounds and could be considered on some occasions as anomic.

Table 1: Descriptive Statistics and Alpha Reliability Coefficient for Response to the Anomie Scale (N=104)

Statement	Possible Responses						
	Strongly Agree	Agree	Disagree	Strongly Disagree	Mean	S.D.
Weighting Value	3	2	1	0		
1. In spite of what people say, the lot of the average man is getting worse.	12.5 (13)	43.3 (45)	33.7 (35)	10.6 (11)	1.58	.844
2. It's hardly fair to bring children into the world with the way things look for the future.	7.7 (8)	44.2 (46)	44.3 (43)	6.7 (7)	1.53	.737
3. Nowadays a person has to live pretty much for today and let tomorrow take care of itself.	21.2 (22)	48.1 (50)	23.1 (24)	7.7 (8)	1.83	.853
4. These days a person doesn't know who he can count on.	19.2 (20)	49.0 (51)	26.9 (28)	4.8 (5)	1.83	.794
5. There's little use writing to public officials because they aren't really interested in the problems of the average man.	3.8 (4)	69.2 (72)	24.0 (25)	2.9 (3)	1.74	.574
6. More and more I feel helpless in the face of what's happening in the world today.	7.7 (8)	30.8 (32)	54.8 (57)	6.7 (7)	1.39	.730
7. There is too much drinking of alcoholic beverages today.	14.4 (15)	36.5 (38)	37.5 (39)	11.5 (12)	1.54	.880
8. People should never smoke marijuana because it leads to a life of drugs.	12.5 (13)	33.7 (35)	27.9 (29)	26.0 (27)	1.33	.999
9. Almost everyone finds leisure time more satisfying than work.	17.3 (18)	52.9 (55)	23.1 (24)	6.7 (7)	1.81	.801
10. Today's sexual morality seems to be, "anything goes."	57.7 (60)	32.7 (34)	9.6 (10)	0.0 (0)	2.48	.666

Items 1-5: Srole (1956); Item 6: Neal and Seeman (1964); Items 7-10: Abrahamson (1980)

The overall mean for the items of the anomie scale for the 104 current and former NFL players is 1.71. This mean represents an overall moderate level of anomie among the athletes. There were 43 players who fell in the low anomie category, 14 who are located in the moderate anomie category, and 47 of the athletes are interpreted to have high levels of anomie. This is consistent with the interview findings in the qualitative data.

The descriptive data for the wealth/aspiration index are presented in Table 2. The data appear to demonstrate that the perception of the importance of wealth and aspiration is a significant factor in many of the players' lives. Wealth/aspiration scores are interpreted as follows: (a) scores of 0-1.59 represent low perceived importance of wealth/aspiration, (b) scores of 1.6-1.99 represent a moderate level of perceived importance of wealth/aspiration, and (c) scores of 2.00-3.00 represent a high level of perceived importance of wealth/aspiration. On the first item, the mean score was 1.91, which indicates that on average a moderate level of players perceived that it is not natural for people to try hard to become wealthy. The second item had a mean of 2.06, revealing that on average a high level of players perceived that it is natural for people to enjoy being wealthy. And the third item had a mean of 2.56, indicating that on average a high level of players in the study group had perceived admiration for people who try to be the best at whatever they do. The data appeared to support the theory and the qualitative findings surrounding the importance of wealth discussed in earlier chapters. The desire to "accumulate wealth and to aspire" reveals a significant change in many of these athletes' lifestyles, as many are instant millionaires after signing NFL contracts. Theoretically, this is consistent with Durkheim's ([1897] 1951) anomie of affluence thesis. According to Durkheim ([1897] 1951), the more one has, the more one aspires to, especially during times of rapid social change and anomic conditions.

Table 2: Descriptive Statistics and Alpha Reliability Coefficient for Response to the Wealth/Aspiration Index (N=104)

Statement	Possible Responses					
	Strongly Agree	Agree	Disagree	Strongly Disagree	Mean	S.D.
Weighting Value	3	2	1	0		
1. It is not natural for people to try hard to become wealthy.	17.3 (18)	58.7 (61)	22.1 (23)	1.9 (2)	1.91	.684
2. It is natural for people to enjoy being wealthy.	26.0 (27)	53.8 (56)	20.2 (20)	0 (0)	2.06	.680
3. I admire people who try to be the best at whatever they do.	59.3 (62)	36.5 (38)	3.8 (4)	0 (0)	2.56	.572

Standardized Item Alpha For Index Reliability = 0.731
Mean Item Score = 2.08
S.D. = 0.547

The data are presented as percentages with frequencies contained with parentheses. The percentages may not sum to 100% due to rounding error. Abrahamson (1980)

The overall item mean of the wealth/attainment index for the 104 current and former NFL players was 2.08. This mean represents an overall high level of aspiration for wealth. There were 22 players who fell in the low wealth/aspiration category, 12 who are located in the moderate wealth/aspiration category, and 70 athletes who had high levels of aspiration for wealth. Again, this is consistent with qualitative data.

The descriptive data for the social ties/support index are presented in Table 3. For the first item, 69 (66.3%), approximately two-thirds of the players, reported having a relationship with God/higher power, while 35 (33.7%) reported not having a relationship with God/higher power. The second item revealed that the athletes' rate of marriage was nearly the same, as 50 (48.1%) or almost half reported being married. As for the other players, 54 (51.9%) reported not being married. The third item disclosed that 67 (64.4%) or nearly two-thirds of the NFL players in the study group had not completed college, while 37 (35.6%) reported having finished college.

Table 3: Descriptive Statistics and Alpha Reliability Coefficient for the Response to the Social Ties/Support Item (N=104)

Statement	Possible Responses			
	Yes	No	Mean	S.D.
Weighting Value	1	0		
1. I have a personal relationship with God/Higher Power.	66.3 (69)	33.7 (35)	.663	.474
2. I am married.	48.1 (50)	51.9 (54)	.48	.508
3. I have graduated from college.	35.6 (37)	64.4 (67)	.36	.481
Standardized Item Alpha For Index Reliability = 0.717 Mean Item = 0.5 S.D. = 0.392				

The data are presented as percentages with frequencies contained in parentheses. The percentages may not sum to 100% due to rounding error.

The overall item mean of the social ties/support index for the 104 current and former NFL players was 0.50. This mean represents, arguably, a fairly moderate level of social ties/support among the players. In essence, approximately half of the players in the study group could be considered to have adequate social ties/support. This is consistent with the qualitative data. Also consistent with the qualitative findings, and with Durkheim's theory, is that those who lack the buffering qualities of social ties/support agents such as religion, marriage, and education are typically more likely to exhibit anomic characteristics.

Descriptive data for the early socialization index are presented in Table 4. In terms of the first item, 66 (63.5%), approximately two-thirds of the players reported being raised in a single parent/guardian household, while 38 (36.5%) reported growing up in a more traditional dual parent/guardian household. For the second item, 65 (62.5%) or nearly two-thirds of the athletes conveyed living in an urban locality for the first ten years of life. On the other hand, 39 (37.5%) reported that they had lived in a rural location for the first ten years of life.

The overall item mean of the early socialization index for the 104 current and former NFL players was 0.63. This mean suggests that relatively few players were raised in a "traditional" environment. In essence, approximately two-thirds of the athletes in the study group could be considered to have received "nontraditional" early socialization. This is consistent with the qualitative findings. Another consistency is that those who grew up in a nontraditional manner appear more likely to experience anomic states.

Because there was variation in the players' attitudes and responses to criminal activity, anomie, and level of happiness, examination of possible explanatory variables and hypothesis testing is warranted. Hypothesis testing was conducted using multiple correlation analysis and the relative explanatory power of the variables was determined by the use of discriminant analysis, logistic regression, and step-wise regression analyses.

Multiple Correlation Analysis

Pearson product moment correlations were calculated for all combinations of variables included in the study for this book and the hypotheses derived from the qualitative data and theory were tested using these coefficients. These data are presented in Table 5. The level of significance

Table 4: Descriptive Statistics and Alpha Reliability Coefficient for Response to the Early Socialization Index (N=104)

Statement	Possible Responses			
	Yes	No	Mean	S.D.
Weighting Value	1	0		
1. I was raised by one or two parents.	Single 63.5 (66)	Two 36.5 (38)	.634	.483
2. How would you describe where you lived for the first ten years of your life?	Urban 62.5 (65)	Rural 37.5 (39)	.625	.486
Standardized Item Alpha For Index Reliability = 0.723 Mean Item = 0.63 S.D. = 0.428				

The data are presented as percentages with frequencies contained in parentheses. The percentages may not sum to 100% due to rounding error.

chosen for hypothesis testing was the 0.01 alpha level. The results of the correlation analysis demonstrate that eight of ten independent variables were significantly correlated with the law abiders/breakers variable at the 0.01 level. The eight variables shown to be significantly related are: anomie, level of happiness, social ties/support, early socialization, counseling/rehabilitation, race, age, and wealth/aspiration. Each of these variables except for one (wealth/aspiration) shown to be significantly related with the law abiders/breakers variable, were correlated in the hypothesized direction. This negative relationship between law abiders/breakers and wealth/aspiration could be interpreted, as those arrested after entrance into the NFL, as being more likely to have less futuristic wealth and aspiration orientations rather than, as originally conceived, simply a great desire for wealth and to aspire (see discussion of anomie scale below for further discussion).

Table 5: Correlation Matrix for Law Breakers Verses Law Abiders, Level of Happiness, and Anomie Scale for Former and Current NFL Players (N=104)

	Law Abiders/ Breakers	Anomie Scale	Level of Happiness	Social Ties/ Support	Early Soc	Income After NFL	Yrs Played	Counseling/ Rehab	Race	Age	Wealth/ Aspiration
Law Abiders/ Breakers	1.00										
Anomie Scale	0.50	1.00									
Level of Happiness	-0.43	-0.64	1.00								
SocialTies/ Support	-0.50	-0.71	0.54	1.00							
Early Soc	0.42	0.64	-0.62	-0.55	1.00						
Income After NFL	0.17*	0.53	-0.40	-0.40	0.42	1.00					
Yrs Played	0.01*	0.00*	0.00*	0.02*	-0.02*	-0.15*	1.00				
Counseling/ Rehab	0.51	0.39	-0.51	-0.40	0.40	0.05*	0.04*	1.00			
Race	0.28	0.40	-0.34	-0.40	0.46	0.13*	-0.04*	0.22	1.00		
Age	-0.45	-0.54	0.38	0.53	-0.25	-0.47	0.18*	-0.20	-0.27	1.00	
Wealth/ Aspiration	-0.42	-0.65	0.35	0.51	-0.38	-0.38	-0.02*	-0.22	-0.23	0.51	1.00

*Not significant at the 0.01 level.

Income after entering the NFL and years played in the NFL were found to have low correlations with the law abiders/breakers variable. The strongest bivariate relationship was between the counseling/rehabilitation variable and the law abiders/breakers variable ($r = 0.51$). It also should be noted that the two other variables with substantial correlations to law abiders/breakers were anomie ($r = 0.50$) and social ties/support ($r = -0.50$).

Nine of the ten independent variables were shown to be significantly correlated with the anomie scale at the 0.01 level. These data are also presented in Table 5. The only independent variable not shown to be significantly related to the anomie scale was years played in the NFL. All but one (wealth/aspiration) of the other independent variables were correlated with the anomie scale in the hypothesized direction. This requires additional interpretation. Originally it was thought that anomie and the study participants' desire for wealth and to aspire would be positively related. But, it could be concluded that this index stresses prescriptive rather than proscriptive (gratification) norms, or in other words, a more futuristic orientation. In essence, this index could be described as emphasizing more traditional attainment orientations, the opposite of what one may expect from an anomic individual who constantly seeks various forms of instant gratification.

Law breakers/abiders ($r = 0.50$), level of happiness ($r = -0.64$), social ties/support ($r = -0.71$), early socialization ($r = 0.64$), income after entering the NFL ($r = 0.53$), age ($r = -0.54$), and wealth/aspiration ($r = -0.65$) displayed moderately strong bivariate relationships to the anomie scale. The magnitude of the correlation coefficients for the anomie scale and the variables of years played in the NFL ($r = 0.00$), counseling/rehabilitation ($r = 0.39$), and race ($r = 0.40$) were relatively low.

Also, nine of the ten independent variables were shown to be significantly related with the level of happiness variable at the 0.01 level. These data are also portrayed in Table 5. The only independent variable that appears to not be significantly correlated to the level of happiness variable was years played in the NFL. All but one (wealth/aspiration) of the other independent variables were correlated with the level of happiness variable in the hypothesized direction. As with the anomie to wealth/aspiration relationship, this negative correlation could be interpreted similarly.

The most substantial bivariate relationship was between anomie and the level of happiness variable ($r = -0.64$). Two other correlations interpreted as moderately strong that also stand out are social ties/support and level of happiness ($r = 0.54$) and counseling/rehabilitation to level of happiness ($r = -0.51$).

In summary, the results of the multiple correlation findings for the law abiders/breakers variable reveal that NFL players in the study group that have been arrested after entrance into the NFL: (1) are likely to exhibit anomic characteristics, (2) are likely to be unhappy, (3) are likely to have few social ties or support networks, (4) are likely to have had a nontraditional early socialization, (5) are likely to have received counseling/rehabilitation, (6) are likely to be younger, (7) are likely to be African-American, and (8) are likely to have less futuristic orientations toward wealth and aspiration. The variables of income after entering the NFL and years played in the NFL were shown not to be significantly related to the law abiders/breakers variable.

The correlational analysis for the anomie scale reveals that those who exhibit anomic characteristics: (1) are likely to have been arrested, (2) are likely to be unhappy, (3) are likely to have inadequate social ties/support, (4) are likely to come from a nontraditional early socialization, (5) are likely to have a higher income, (6) are likely to have received counseling or rehabilitation, (7) are likely to be African-American, (8) are likely to be younger, and (9) are likely to have less futuristic orientations toward wealth/aspiration. Years played in the NFL was not significantly related to the anomie scale.

For the level of happiness variable, the correlational analysis shows that those who are unhappy with life (1) are likely to have been arrested, (2) are likely to be anomic, (3) are likely to have few social ties or support systems, (4) are likely to come from nontraditional early socialization backgrounds, (5) are likely have a higher income, (6) are likely to have received counseling/rehabilitation, (7) are likely to be African-American, (8) are likely to be younger, and (9) are likely to have negligible futuristic orientations toward wealth/aspiration. Years played in the NFL was not significantly correlated to the level of happiness variable.

Discriminant Analysis for Law-Abiding Versus Law-Breaking Players

The data in this study were analyzed using discriminant analysis in order to differentiate between law abiders and law breakers. Discriminant analysis is recognized for the statistical ability to classify by differentiating variables (Klecka 1975). These data are presented in Table 6. In order to differentiate between law abiders and law breakers, the discriminant calculation was performed. The larger the coefficient, the larger the value of that factor in discriminating between the two groups. For this reason, the size of the coefficient is the primary concern, not whether it is positive or negative.

As shown in Table 6, counseling/rehabilitation, age, and anomie are the three factors that most differentiate law abiders from law breakers. Social ties/support, early socialization, wealth/attainment, income, years played in the NFL, level of happiness, and race were relatively non-differentiated factors. In the discriminant calculation the canonical correlation was 0.645, eigenvalue was 0.71, and the chi-square was 54.1 at the 0.001 significance level. In essence, players from the study group appear to have a greater probability of being law breakers if they have the following characteristics: (1) they have received counseling or rehabilitation services, (2) they are younger, and (3) they are anomic.

Logistic Regression Analysis for Law-Abiding Versus Law-Breaking Players

The data in this study were also analyzed using logistic regression in order to verify findings from the discriminant analysis. This was deemed important due to empirical findings that discriminant analysis has been "found to be generally inferior, although not always by substantial amounts" (Press & Wilson 1978: 699). In logistic regression, a predictive equation is developed that is formulated to use the best combination of predictors rather than considering just one factor at a time. The logistic regression findings for law abiders/breakers are presented in Table 6.

Logistic regression analysis was performed using a stepwise selection method. Of the 104 current and former NFL players in the study group, 33 were arrested after entering the NFL. The logistic regression analysis for this group resulted in the development of an equation in which three variables made significant contributions to predictive power:

Table 6: Logistic Regression and Discriminant Analysis for Law Abiding Versus Law Breaking Players After Their Entrance Into the NFL (N=104)

	Best Model Logistic Regression: Three Steps						
Step	Variables	B	S.E.	Wald	D.F.	Sig.	R^2
1	Counseling/Rehab	-2.32	.650	12.837	1	.001	.223
2	Age	-.263	.103	6.474	1	.011	.362
3	Anomie Scale	1.285	.641	4.020	1	.045	.390
	Constant	6.055	3.768	2.583	1	.108	
	Chi Square for Model = 51.35 D.F. = 3 Sig. = .001						

	Best Model Discriminant Analysis: Three Steps				
Step	Variables	Standardized Canonical Discriminant Coefficient	Wilks Lamda	F	Sig.
1	Counseling/Rehab	.652	.737	36.40	.001
2	Age	-.457	.614	31.72	.001
3	Anomie Scale	.388	.583	23.79	.001
Eigenvalue = 0.71 Canonical Correlation = .645					
Chi Square = 54.15					
Sig. = .001					

Variables Entered Into the Analyses:	
Anomie Scale	Level of Happiness
Social Ties/Support Index	Counseling/Rehabilitation
Early Socialization Index	Race
Income	Age
Yrs Played in the NFL	Wealth/Aspiration Index

(1) counseling/rehabilitation, (2) age, and (3) anomie. In the logistic regression calculation, the r^2 was 0.390 and the chi-square was 51.35 at the 0.001 significance level. In essence, as found from the discriminant analysis, players appear to have a higher probability of being law breakers if they have the following characteristics: (1) they have received counseling or rehabilitation, (2) they are younger, and (3) they are anomic.

Regression Analysis

Step-wise multiple regression analysis was conducted on the data to determine the relative explanatory power of the independent variables when all were considered simultaneously. The variance in the anomie scale was regressed against the ten independent variables chosen from qualitative data and theory for the purpose of building the best (maximum explained variance) explanatory model. The best model is presented below in standardized regression coefficient form (beta) using the multiple linear regression equation:

$$y = B_1 x_1 + B_2 x_2 \ldots B_n x_n + e$$

where:
y = dependent variable
B = standardized regression coefficient (beta)
x = score on independent variable
e = residual error

The regression findings for the anomie scale are presented in Table 7. Five variables were shown to be significant in reducing the unexplained variance in the dependent variable. The five-variable model explained 71.4% of the variance in the anomie scale variable. The best regression model is presented below in standardized partial regression coefficient form:

$$y = -0.710 x_1 - 0.393 x_2 - 0.325 x_3 + 0.204 x_4 + 0.130 x_5 + e$$

where:
x_1 = Social Ties/Support
x_2 = Wealth/Aspiration
x_3 = Level of Happiness
x_4 = Early Socialization
x_5 = Income after NFL
e = Residual error

Discriminant Analysis for Happy Versus Unhappy Players

Due to qualitative findings and multiple regression findings, I reasoned it appropriate to also analyze the data using discriminant analysis in order to differentiate between happy and unhappy players. As shown in Table 8, study participants appear to have a higher probability of being unhappy (1) if they are anomic, (2) if they were raised in a nontraditional manner during their early socialization, and (3) if they have received counseling or rehabilitation. For the discriminant analysis, the canonical correlation was 0.735, the eigenvalue was 1.18, and the chi-square was 78.16 at the 0.001 significance level.

Table 7: Step-Wise Regression for Anomie Scale with Current and Former NFL Players Presented in Standardized Regression Coefficient Form (N=104)

Step	Social Ties/ Support Index	Wealth/ Aspiration Index	Level of Happiness	Early Socialization	Income After NFL	Adjusted R^2	F Ratio or Entering Variable	Level of Significance
1	-.710					.500	103.86	.001
2	-.510	-.393				.611	81.94	.001
3	-.351	-.361	-.325			.684	75.22	.001
4	-.297	-.343	-.233	.204		.704	62.20	.001
5	-.281	-.317	-.213	.180	.130	.714	52.41	.001

Variables not Entering: Law Abiders versus Law Breakers, Age, Race, Counseling/Rehabilitation, Yrs Played NFL

Table 8: Logistic Regression and Discriminant Analysis for Happy Versus Unhappy with Life (N=104)

	Best Model Logistic Regression: Three Steps						
Step	Variables	B	S.E.	Wald	D.F.	Sig.	R^2
1	Anomie Scale	-2.43	.712	11.69	1	.001	.395
2	Early Soc Index	-.284	1.02	7.64	1	.006	.475
3	Counseling/ Rehab	2.01	.80	6.212	1	.013	.512
	Constant	5.17	1.65	9.77	1	.002	
Chi Square for Model = 74.62 D.F. = 3 Sig. = .001							

	Best Model Discriminant Analysis: Three Steps			
Step	Variables	Standardized Canonical Discriminant Coefficient	Wilks Lamda	F Sig.
1	Anomie Scale	.536	.591	70.55 .001
2	Early Soc Index	.464	.508	48.87 .001
3	Counseling/Rehab	.446	.459	39.21 .001
Eigenvalue =1.18 Canonical Correlation=.735 Chi Square =78.16 Sig. = .001				

Variables Entered Into the Analyses:	
Anomie Scale	Counseling/Rehabilitation
Social Ties/Support Index	Race
Early Socialization Index	Age
Income	Wealth/Aspiration Index
Yrs Played in the NFL	

Logistic Regression Analysis for Happy Versus Unhappy Players

Again, in order to verify findings from the discriminant analysis, data were analyzed using logistic regression (See Table 8). Of the 104 players in the study group, 46 reported being unhappy with life. Similar to the discriminant analysis, respondents appear to have a greater probability of being unhappy (1) if they are anomic, (2) if they were brought up in a nontraditional manner during their early socialization, and (3) if they have received counseling/rehabilitation. For this "best" model, the r^2 was 0.512 and the chi-square was 74.62 significant beyond the 0.001 level.

Synopsis of Quantitative Findings

A synopsis of the research findings is presented below:

A) First, the responses to the dependent variable, law abiders/breakers, indicates that approximately one-third of the players have been arrested after their entrance into the NFL. Second, the responses to the dependent variable, anomie, reveal that an alarming 45 percent of the athletes are interpreted to exhibit various anomic characteristics. Third, the responses to the dependent variable, level of happiness, suggest that nearly half of the players in the study group are unhappy with life. The descriptive statistics appear to indicate that social ties/support and socialization factors have significant buffering qualities in relation to anomie and deviance. Also, age appears to be an important variable, as those who are younger seem less able to cope with stressful life change than do the older athletes in the study sample.

B) The bivariate correlations indicate that the socio-demographic variable of years played in the NFL was, largely, a poor predictor of law abiders/breakers, anomie, and level of happiness. The other ten variables appear to be important correlates of the three dependent variables. Overall, there appears to be a relationship between anomie, level of happiness, and law abiders/breakers. These variables also appear to be associated to social ties/support, early socialization, income,

counseling/rehabilitation, age, and wealth/aspiration (future attainment orientations).
C) First, the multivariate statistics indicate that the independent variables of counseling/rehabilitation, age, and anomie appear to be important predicting variables of law abiders/breakers. Second, the multivariate statistics reveal that the independent variables of social ties/support, wealth/aspiration, level of happiness, early socialization, and income after the NFL appear to be important correlates of anomie. Third, the multivariate statistics indicate that the independent variables of anomie, early socialization, and counseling/rehabilitation appear to be important predictors of a player's level of happiness. The socio-demographic variable of years played in the NFL was generally a poor predictor of the three dependent variables.

References

Abrahamson, Mark. 1980. Sudden wealth, gratification and attainment: Durkheim's anomie of affluence reconsidered. *American Sociological Review* 45: 49-57.

Durkheim, Emile. [1897] 1951. *Suicide*. Trans. John A. Spaulding and George Simpson. New York: Free Press.

Klecka, William R. 1975. Discriminant analysis. In *SPSS: Statistical package for the social sciences*, 2nd ed. Eds. Norman Nie, Hadlai Hull, Jean Jenkins, Karin Steinbrenner and Dale Bent, 434-467. New York: McGraw Hill.

Neal, Arthur G., and Melvin Seeman. 1964. Organizations and powerlessness. *American Sociological Review* 29: 216-226.

Press, James S., and Sandra Wilson. 1978. Choosing between logistic regression and discriminant analysis. *Journal of the American Statistical Association* 73: 699-705.

Srole, Leo. 1956. Social integration and certain corollaries: An exploratory study. *American Sociological Review* 21: 709-716.

Chapter Nine

Key Considerations for the Future: Social Control or Empowerment?

This research for this book set out to explore three key questions: (1) What are the factors associated with law breaking behavior for NFL players in the study group? (2) Can levels of anomie be identified among NFL players in the study sample, and if so, what factors are associated with anomie? and (3) Do the law breakers exhibit anomic characteristics?

Counseling/rehabilitation, age, and anomie were found to be the discriminating variables in identifying who had participated in illegal behaviors—by being been arrested since becoming professional football players—versus those who had not. These variables suggested that those who had received counseling/rehabilitation services, those who were younger, and those who possessed higher scores on the anomie scale were more likely to be law breakers within this group of players studied. These findings were confirmed through both discriminant analysis and logistic regression analysis and were very consistent with the findings from the qualitative data. The qualitative data revealed multiple instances where the presence of counseling and rehabilitation, the younger less experienced, and those who were having a difficult time because of the changes brought about by becoming professional football players were involved in some type of deviant behavior.

Although the concept of anomie is complex, Durkheim's detailed and comprehensive insight provides a theoretical perspective by which the life circumstances affecting these players can be conceptualized and described. Durkheim's work may date back 100 years, but his keen insight into the effects of rapid social change continues to provide a useful theoretical model. His development of the sociological concept of anomie, even today provides a theoretical, yet empirically testable, perspective for explaining social deviance. I would go so far as to suggest that with the information explosion of today's digital age, Durkheim may be even more relevant and important as social scientists attempt to explain the effect of social change on any number of social groups. Durkheim needs to be "rediscovered" and the research on anomie expanded if we are to have "sociological definitions" of the impact and result of social change.

The results of this study suggest that the sudden wealth (rapid change) of many players was associated at varying levels with these players' personal anomie. The findings indicate when higher levels of anomie are present: (1) weaker social ties and fewer forms of support have been experienced by the players, (2) players possess less of a commitment to future aspirations and the investment in the attainment of wealth, (3) players are unhappy with life, (4) less constructive and productive agents of early socialization were present in the lives of the players, (5) they earned a higher income since becoming a professional football player compared to lesser earning players, and (6) higher levels of deviant and sometimes unlawful behavior were a part of their lives compared to law-abiding and less deviant players.

Interestingly, the findings suggest that sudden wealth produces an increase in gratification acceptance and a decrease in future attainment orientations for this group of players. These results appear to be congruent with Durkheim's ([1897] 1951) anomie of affluence thesis. Durkheim ([1897] 1951) noted that when rapid change occurs, social bonds are weakened, thus exciting "fevered imaginations" (256). Also, compatible with Durkheimian theory, is the observed relationship between size of income and anomie. As wealth was acquired, so too was an increase in anomic characteristics. Thus, qualitative findings do support the Durkheimian thesis and the direction of these measured associations. In the interviews, player after player spoke of early socialization experiences, or lack thereof, and gave graphic explanations of how the NFL had created a life they were not ready to experience.

Closely associated to the theoretical construct of anomie is the level of happiness or unhappiness found within players in the study group. Anomie, early socialization, and counseling/rehabilitation were the significant predictors of whether a player was happy or unhappy with life. These variables imply that those who exhibited anomic characteristics, those that were raised in nontraditional early socialization structures, and those who had received counseling or rehabilitation services were more likely to be unhappy with their current life situation. As with law abiders/breakers, these findings were confirmed through discriminant analysis and logistic regression analysis. They, too, were fully consistent with the qualitative data. The degree of unhappiness among players interviewed was one of the most surprising findings from the interviews. Although this was a snowball sample, the implications posed by the degree of unhappiness mentioned in the interviews leads me to believe this is a widespread social psychological state of being for many NFL players.

Notable Findings

There were several findings that appear to stand out and are worth noting from the research conducted for this book. First, anomie was one of the significant predictors of law breaking players (players who were arrested). It would appear that anomie plays at least a partial role in whether some of these athletes fall victim to the correlates that accompany deviant behavior. For this study group, 47 of the 104 (45%) players reported moderate to high levels of anomie as it was operationalized and measured. It would therefore appear reasonable to suggest that some of the players in the study group were involved in behaviors and activities that could be labeled as *anomic deviance*. As Durkheim ([1897] 1951) suggested, there are different types of deviance (suicide). This type—anomic—characterizes the social state that leads to this particular type of deviance. Further, the anomic social state of a group or condition is thus identified as an explanation of personal anomie. This finding suggests the continued applicability of Durkheimian theory even as applied to the lives of players in the National Football League today.

A second finding that stands out was that nearly half of the study group reported being unhappy with life, a high percentage when compared to the American population in general and to many occupational work groups in particular (Saad 2004). Anomie was also the strongest predictor of unhappiness for players in the study group. With the early socialization index also being a highly associated correlate, this indicated that prior socialization factors played some role in how players adapted to the rapidly changing environment of professional football. Qualitative findings gave support and additional validity to these findings.

The third interesting dimension to this study was the methodological approach developed and used to gather these data. The fact that a high degree of compatibility was found between the qualitative data and quantitative data was important with regard to reliability and validity of the research. The categories discovered through the qualitative field data were supported when operationalized and tested through the quantitative analyses.

The technique of elite and specialized interviews made the other data available for the study. No data would be available had it not been for the help of the two key informants. In other words, valid and reliable information from some social groups, as was the case for player information out of the NFL, is virtually impossible to obtain without informants who provide entrée into the closed group.

This book raises many questions about sudden life and economic change, anomie, and deviant behavior when they occur in the lives of professional football players and, even beyond, in other groups which experience rapid professional and personal change. Variables could be, and need to be, refined so as to measure more accurately the essential concepts and constructs surrounding anomie, social ties/support, early socialization, wealth/aspiration, and the influence of fame, power, and money in professional football. Additional dimensions need to be explored in the creation of the anomie scale and other indices. Certainly, the research carried out for this book is just one step of several in improving the methodology for validity, reliability, and degree of representativeness of the life characteristics of professional football players.

Suggestions and Possible Applied Action Steps Supported by the Research

I would argue, based on the research findings and theory, that the rapid life change players encounter going from college to the professional ranks will always be there. In essence, there will always be various levels of anomie in the lives of NFL players as a result of being suddenly wealthy. However, as reported in this study, social support, in many cases, can be a key buffer against this anomie. Thus, various social groups and institutions must emerge, and become manifest in the lives of these athletes, in order to provide the necessary relationships and support they are in desperate need of. In many cases, not only is integration and regulation needed but re-socialization becomes a key factor.

First, colleges and universities, it appears from these data, do not do enough to ground and socialize their student-athletes or prepare them for life after college. I would argue that there needs to be a greater effort on the part of colleges and universities to help these young men acquire life-skills and to teach socialization skills to their many at-risk athletes (those from low socio-economic backgrounds, poor schools, and broken-homes). Many of these athletes' lives revolve only around being football players. In other words, many of these athletes have not been taught how to deal with typical everyday situations such as relationships, anger, and personal issues. Some athletes have not acquired the socialization skills that many people outside of high-profile athletics learn. Their lives are football. They learn how to play hard and hit hard. And, in too many cases, socialization skills are not being taught by the athletes' families or guardians due to backgrounds full of violence, broken-homes, and various other unfortunate situations. Thus, colleges and universities need to add and emphasize a student-athlete life skills curriculum. Too many of these young men enter the professional ranks without "education." The majority never graduate from college and some are barely literate. The lack of adequate education can have detrimental effects on many players' decision-making ability and their ability to cope with drastic life and economic change.

Second, the data suggest that NFL teams need to show more support. At-risk players need to be provided additional support and structure by their teams and coaches. Coping mechanisms need to be instilled early in these athletes' careers. And, if players deviate (or break the law) consistently they need to be placed on suspension and required to undergo rehabilitation or further life-skills training. This suspension should not be deemed necessarily as disciplinary, but rather viewed as an opportunity for players to acquire further and more in-depth life skills. For this to be successful, teams must hire more professional personnel with the expertise to assist these athletes in coping with their changing lives. This staff would also be able to offer support and help empower players—in essence, emphasizing empowerment instead of social control. However, "character clauses" should be in players' contracts (most teams have something of this nature in player contracts but rarely enforce it) and they need to be taken seriously. Teams need to stress the risks and consequences associated with illegal conduct, especially crimes against women. But, again, teams must above all support their players, empower their players, and equip their players with the life skills necessary for daily life during and after their professional careers. With the proper encouragement and support, much of the enforcement may not be needed.

If staff better understands the culture their athletes are enmeshed in, they will be better able to identify with their players' life situations and personal issues, allowing them to offer proper support.

Third, if teams are unwilling to set some standards, help players acquire necessary coping skills, and support their players, then perhaps the NFL as a league may need to step in and develop consistent policies and support structures. The NFL commissioner has recently taken new disciplinary steps to address player conduct, but needs to offer more support and skills development for teams and players, and, more importantly, help these young men adjust to all the life changes that occur as a result of becoming wealthy and famous professional athletes. The NFL has policies dealing with criminal and various other forms of deviant behavior such as drug use and gambling, but those largely disciplinary policies appear not to be working. The league is relatively reactive instead of proactive in this respect. My data indicate that the NFL needs to help at-risk players at the front end of their careers and provide them with adequate support, perhaps even mandatory support. And instead of simply trying to discipline and control players, the league needs to act more proactively towards player empowerment during the early stages of their careers.

Furthermore, the commissioner may need to work more closely with outside organizations and the player's union in order to further protect the athletes. The NFL needs to insist that *all* agents (and various others) meet professional standards and protect their clients. The league should also require similar standards for the managers and coaches. According to the findings from this study, many players enter the NFL in a very vulnerable condition. They must be protected and given adequate opportunity to succeed. However, the data also suggest that many players require some structure or sense of boundaries. Otherwise, deviance can be reproduced (especially if support is weak), as was the case for many of the players in the study group. In essence, the NFL needs consistency in policy, but more importantly, consistency in support and empowerment.

Additionally, and in fairness to the NFL, the problem of deviance and unlawful behavior among players did not come about overnight, but is largely structural in nature. Deviance and criminal behavior in our society and the NFL are complex social problems, much too multifaceted and complicated for the NFL alone to solve. However, the commissioner and teams are not powerless to address much of the problem within their organizations. The commissioner, team owners, and managers, I would argue, can reduce the occurrence of deviance and illegal behavior among players. Support must be consistent. And it appears that there needs to be less emphasis simply on "discipline." According to one player, "Most guys laugh off fines. . . . let me tell you, fines don't stop players from doing anything. Suspensions . . . now *that* hurts us more [because] . . . that's what we do, we love to play . . . but, let me say again, that kind of stuff doesn't affect us that much."

Moreover, the research findings point toward further suggestions for how to combat the anomic and often deviant behavior of NFL players. Based on the data, I would argue, in addition to the suggestions above, that (1) to better prepare the athletes for what they will encounter in relation to sudden life change, the NFL needs to have more in-depth conversations with the NCAA and universities/colleges concerning the issues surrounding the drastic life change that occurs upon players' entrance into the NFL; (2) players need more education, perhaps programs that assist them in finishing their college degrees, or at the very least, require in- and off-season workshops focused on acquiring additional life skills and coping mechanisms; (3) team, league, and societal rules and laws should be recognized (for all players, even the superstars), as too many players in the study group reported "no consequences;" (4) there needs to be more support and accountability during the non-playing or practicing times and during the off-season, as too many players indicated that they were "bored;" (5) a more formal "buddy system" needs to be instituted whereby responsible veteran or team alumni assist the young players (rookies), help them adjust to their new life, support them, and empower them, essentially, giving them a positive peer relationship; (6) there needs to be more meaningful "charity" displayed by players who, according to one player, "have the resources to make a difference;" and (7) there needs to be more help for the players in coping with their sudden wealth and fame at the front end, or when they enter the league, rather than just that provided at the back end, or when they retire (which, as suggested by several players, is not very good either). See Table 1 for a proposed model for player enhancement and success.

Table 1: A Proposed Model for Player Enhancement and Success

Goal: To sustain players who will be *successful* not only on the field but off of the field.

Manifest Goal: Successful at Life—Sense of Purpose
Latent Goal: Success at Football
Research Strategy: Assess level of player anomie or ability to adjust and cope with life in the NFL.

Phase One

Screen players at draft or other selection times using instrument which scores/ranks players on key indicators. (A careful methodology must be utilized to obtain validity and reliability).

Phase Two

Re-test for more specific information so as to develop appropriate player enhancement Plan.

Phase Three

Develop and implement individualized plan for success.

Phase Four

Implement professional development model for entire organization. A higher probability of success if the culture of the organization supports the player changes being implemented.

Assumptions of the model:

- ➢ People/players are fairly integrated in terms of attitudes and behaviors. If people are successful in one aspect of life they can obtain success in another. The same is true for negative behaviors. The need is to create more positive behavior than negative for players.

- Player success must be built upon positive attributes and behaviors.
- Use of effective mentors is beneficial and builds trust, happiness, sharing and collegiality for team.
- Sense of purpose through service is key. People find themselves by sharing and doing for others. The benefits of *service to others* are manifold.

A consistent statement that I heard from NFL personnel was that "we cannot make them [their players] do anything." I would argue that they cannot *make* their players "do anything" (especially outside of work) but they can empower them by providing them with the tools necessary to be successful, both professionally and off the field. And regardless of their fame, players are employees of an organization that could and should, to some degree, hold players accountable for breaking team and league rules, as well as breaking the law. Therefore, there should be, as in other professional organizations, a code of conduct for athletes privileged enough to get paid millions of dollars to play sports (football). Some of this is starting to be done, as when Minnesota Vikings owner Zygi Wilf delivered a 77-page code of conduct to his team in response to the "sex boat" scandal during the 2005 season. However, it appears to have had little effect on some Viking's players (or is not being enforced for certain star players) as there were several mishaps during the 2006 preseason. But again this accountability and these conduct codes need to be implemented by enhancing support instead of enforcement. In essence, while there does need to be some regulation, one could argue that the key to combating anomie and deviance lies in social support, skills development, education, and empowerment.

And, perhaps, if player deviance were acknowledged from the perspective of helping and educating players who have made bad decisions, and social support made widely available for players with personal issues, teams might perform at higher levels simply because there would be fewer distractions and less negative media attention. This has the potential to increase winning percentages for teams and an enhanced public image for the NFL. As my data consistently show, if players do not have social support available to them, the outcome frequently is player deviance, team turmoil, and, as some NFL personnel told me, potentially bad investments for team owners.[1] This was largely the case for many of the players in the study group and the various others that commented on the current state of deviance in the NFL.

Future Research

There are numerous ways future research could and should be pursued. With broader access to NFL players, a more comprehensive research project could be undertaken. Future research pertaining to the above-applied action steps could lend further insight into improving the life of NFL players. Helping team management and coaches understand and assist players in coping with the affects of sudden fame and fortune, might help to reduce the anomic deviance and unhappiness which was found in both the qualitative and quantitative findings. Players spoke often of the inability to cope with their emotional pain and suffering since becoming professional football players. An area that needs to be addressed is the degree of influence many of the players bring from prior socialization and life experience. This prior set of experiences appeared to play a role in the presence of anomie and level of happiness. The data indicated that early socialization and the role of social ties were very important predictors of anomie and deviance for this study group. Also, the increasing role of religion as a social bond appeared to have a significant influence in players' lives. Further examination of that phenomenon is warranted. Hence, a more comprehensive model for explaining anomic deviance is needed.

Most people are aware that there are problems in the NFL. According to Lapchick (2000), "Our athletes are coming from a generation of despairing youth cut adrift from the American Dream" (15). In other words, many young athletes are coming from early socialization experiences that entail "balancing life and death" (Lapchick 2000: 15). NFL teams are drafting players who have (1) increasingly observed the violent death of friends, peers, and family members, (2) who are fathers before they reach the NFL, (3) who have witnessed drug abuse by friends and family, (4) who have witnessed abuse and battering in their own homes, and (5) who were raised in a single parent or guardian household (Lapchick 2000). Thus, universities/colleges and the NFL need professionals who can deal with all of these unfortunate factors and can aid in "re-socializing" these athletes. However, according to players in the study group, few teams are equipped with people that can help guide and support them throughout their professional careers. Thus, I would argue that these elements of early socialization warrant further research.

The present research indicated factors of importance to NFL players, better understanding of which could potentially assist owners, coaches, players, and the general public in appreciating their effects—factors that need to be understood more completely through theoretical study and further research. Although this study focused on only a small number of NFL players, there is a phenomenon here larger than the one Durkheim ([1897] 1951) pointed out over 100 years ago. When the rules of life change rapidly, many people have difficulty adjusting. In many cases, if people do not have social ties and support during life-changing events, anomie and deviance can result. This normative breakdown can be present in many venues other than professional football. There should be a fresh discovery of Durkheim's insight on social change. Anomie should be viewed as a very important perspective to explore and apply in new and emerging instances in the twenty-first century. It is my hope that this book can help reignite inquiry into rapid life change, anomie, and deviance as well as generate meaningful discussion about the current state of professional football and the athletes who are the participants in this sport.

Note

1. As my data suggest, social support is essential is helping professional football players cope with their instant financial success. Without it, players are likely to engage in deviant forms of behavior as a way to handle newfound pressures associated with rapid life changes. The data suggest that player empowerment through various methods of social support can not only help them deal with their rapidly changing lives, but also provide them with more opportunities for future success in life. But, as the current situation reflects, the NFL and team owners would rather *control* players rather than *empower* them. An important question remains: Why? Are there advantages to keeping players anomic and disempowered? It must be noted that several players reported feeling like slaves on an auction block. They recognized how they are commodities that are bought and sold in the marketplace. They acknowledged that they made a lot of money, but also acknowledged that they made even more money for their wealthy owners. In essence, there are larger structures and assumptions that must be challenged if professional football players, particularly African-

American players, are going to be afforded consistent support by the NFL. Future research will be important for answering these lingering questions.

References

Durkheim, Emile. [1897] 1951. *Suicide*. Trans. John A. Spaulding and George Simpson. New York: Free Press.

Lapchick, Richard E. 2000. Crime and athletes: New racial stereotypes. *Society* 37: 14-20.

Saad, Lydia. 2004. A nation of happy people. *Gallup News Service*. <http://www.freepublic.com/focus/f-news/1051689/posts>. Retrieved July 6, 2006.

Index

Note to Index: An *f* following a page number indicates a figure on that page; a *t* following a page number indicates a table on that page.

A
age, as variable, 86
alcohol abuse, 47, 48, 49
anomic suicide, 20
anomie: acute anomic currents in football, 26–27; acute anomie, 25–26; chronic anomic currents in football, 23–25; chronic anomie, 23; conceptual model of, 17–18*f*; defining, 3, 4–5, 16–17; division of labor and, 19; Durkheim's conception of, 10, 12, 14, 18–22; forms of, 23; key aspects of, 29; personal anomie, 27; social psychological level of, 28–29; as state of deregulation, 20–21; strain theory, 12–13. *see also* anomie patterns; anomie scale
anomie of affluence thesis, 96
anomie patterns, 55–60; happy *vs.* unhappy with life, 57–60; ideal-typical anomie, 59–60; sudden wealth and status change, 55–57. *see also* anomie
anomie scale, 93–99, 95*t*; reliability analysis, of scales/indices, 87*t*; response to attitude items, 93–99; response to wealth/aspiration index, 97*t*; social ties/support item, 98*t*
arrest: deviance without arrest, 49–51; police deference and, 48–49; statistics on, 5

B
Bellah, Robert, 2
Benedict, Jeff, 5, 6
Bernard, Thomas J., 12
blaming the victim, 47
blended research, 35. *see also* field research
Blumstein, Alfred, 5

C
Caplan, Gerald, 16
Cassel, John, 16
Chicago School, 15–16
childhood family dynamics, 67–68
childhood friends, 69–70
civil religion, 2
Cobb, Sidney, 16
Cohen, Harry, 27
collective consciousness, 15, 19

C

commodification, of athletes, 2–3, 26–27
conformity, 14
counseling/rehabilitation, 51–52, 85
Cullen, Francis T., 16
cult figure, athlete as, 26–27

D

dependent variables, 78–83; anomie, 81–83; attitude anomie scale/weighting, 82t; attitude index, 84t–86t; early socialization, 86t; happy vs. unhappy with life, 83; law abiders vs. law breakers, 81; social ties/support, 85t; wealth-aspiration, 84t
deviance patterns, 45–53; behavior categories, 45f; deviance without arrest, 49–51; ideal-typical deviance, 52–53; law-breaking behavior, 46–48; police deference and arrest, 48–49; rehabilitation/counseling, 51–52
Dexter, Louis, 6, 36, 37
differential association theory, 12
discriminant analysis, 90, 91; happy vs. unhappy with life, 107, 109t; law-abiding vs. law-breaking players, 104; law abiding vs. law breaking players, 105t
division of labor, 18–19
domestic violence, 49, 50
drug abuse, 47, 48, 49, 50; rehabilitation, 51–52
Durkheim, Emile, 2, 4–5, 113–114; on acute anomie, 25–26, 27; anomie of affluence thesis, 96; on chronic anomie, 23, 24–25; conception of anomie, 10, 12, 14, 17, 18–22, 28; on human wants and desires, 15; suicide study, 10, 15, 19–21; on types of anomie, 115

E

early socialization: childhood family dynamics, 67–68; childhood friends, 69–70; dependent variables, 86t; ideal-typical social ties/support, 70–72; independent variables, 85; index, 89t, 115; socioeconomic status, 68; urban/rural location, 69
eccentric social environment, 5–6
economic depression, 26
educational background, 64
elite/specialized interview, 36, 116

F

family, 63–64
field research, 35; acceptance by players, 39–41; core themes of stories, 42–43; evidence of deviance, 42–43f; factors influencing, 43f; in-depth interviews, 41–42; indications of anomie, 42–43f; key informants, 36, 38–39; social ties, 42–43f; working behavioral/attitudinal model, 43f
forced division of labor, 19
franchise revenues, 24
future considerations, 113–124; research, 122–123; suggestions/applied action steps, 116–122

H

happy vs. unhappy with life, 57–60, 74–75, 109t, 110, 115
Hirschi, Travis, 14–15

I

ideal-typical anomie, 59–60
ideal-typical deviance, 52–53
ideal-typical social ties/support, 70–72

Index 127

income, 24, 85–86
independent variables, 83–86; age, 86; counseling/rehabilitation, 85; early socialization, 85; income (after entering NFL), 85–86; social ties/support, 84–85; wealth/aspiration, 83–84; years played in NFL, 86
institutional discrimination, 72n2
instrument construction, 77
interview, elite/specialized, 36, 116
iron cage, 28

K
key informants, 36, 38–39, 76, 77
Klecka, William R., 90
Kornhauser, Ruth R., 13

L
Labovitz, Sanford, 90
Lapchick, Richard E., 122
law-abiding vs. law-breaking players, 46–48, 74, 81, 101t, 104–106, 105t
Lin, Nan, 16
logistic regression analysis, 90, 91; happy vs. unhappy with life, 109t, 110; law-abiding vs. law-breaking players, 104–106, 105t

M
MacIver, Robert, 28
macro-level analysis, 10
marriage, 63
means-needs balance, 25
mechanical solidarity, 18, 19
media: "American Dream" and, 2–3; television, 2, 3, 24
Merton, Robert, 12
micro-level analysis, 10
multiple correlation analysis, 90, 99–103; early socialization index, 100t; law breakers vs. abiders/

happiness/anomie scale, 101t
multiple regression analysis, 90, 91
mythic figures, athletes as, 2–3

N
naturalistic research, 6, 35

O
open-ended research, 35
ordered-metric scale, 90
organic solidarity, 18–19
Orru, Marco, 17, 28

P
parametric statistical analysis, 89–90
Parsons, Talcott, 17, 20, 28
Passas, Nikos, 28
Paul, Benjamin D., 36
peers, 65
personal anomie, 27
player enhancement and success, proposed model, 120t
Pope, Whitney, 25, 26
Powell, Elwin H., 30
prostitution, 5, 46, 48, 49, 53
pseudo-religion, football as, 2

Q
qualitative research: data collection phases, 36–37f; research questions/generalized observations, 73–74. *see also* quantitative research
quantitative research, 76–78; characteristics of sample, 78; sample selection, 77; structured questionnaire, 77; study situation, 76. *see also* qualitative research; quantitative variables/hypotheses
quantitative variables/hypotheses, 74–76; anomie, 74; early socialization, 75; happy with life

vs. unhappy with life, 74–75; hypotheses synthesized, 75–76; law-abiding *vs.* law-breaking players, 74; social ties/support, 75; wealth and aspiration, 75

R
racism, 72n2
regression analysis, 106, 108*t*; logistic, 90, 91, 104–106, 105*t*, 109*t*–110; multiple, 90, 91
rehabilitation/counseling, 51–52, 85
reliability analysis, of scales/indices, 86–89, 116; anomie scale, 87*t*; early socialization index, 89*t*; social ties/support index, 88*t*; wealth/aspiration index, 88*t*
religion, 64–64
research findings, 93–111; discriminant analysis, 104, 107; logistic regression analysis, 104–106, 109*t*, 110; multiple correlation analysis, 99–103; notable findings, 115–116; regression analysis, 106; response to attitude items, 93–99; step-wise regression, 108*t*; synopsis of, 110–111
research questions/generalized observations, 73–74
Riesman, David, 28
role models, 3, 5
Rozelle, Pete, 2, 24

S
sample, research: characteristics of, 78; selection of, 77
Samuels, Allison, 4
Schatzman, Leonard, 6, 35–36
separation anxiety, 17
sexual misconduct, 46–47, 50, 52–53, 55*f*
snowball sampling, 77

social bond, 14
social change, rate of, 20
social control theory, 10, 14–15
social disorganization theory, 9–10, 14–30, 29; social control theory, 10, 14–15; social psychological level of anomie, 28–29; social support theory, 15–16. *see also* anomie; subcultural learning theory
social facts, 20
social psychological level of anomie, 28–29
social support and ties: dependent variables, 85*t*; independent variables, 84–85; quantitative variables and hypotheses, 75; reliability analysis, of scales/indices, 88*t*. *see also* early socialization; social support/control
social support/control, 61–65; educational background, 64; family, 63–64; marriage, 63; peers, 65; religion, 64–65
social support theory, 15–16
social ties theme, 62*f*
socioeconomic status, 68
Sports Broadcasting Act, 24
Srole, Leo, 28
Starr, Mark, 4
statistical analyses, 89–91
statistics, descriptive, 79*t*–80*t*
stereotypes, negative, 1
strain theory, 12–13
Strauss, Anselem, 6, 35–36
structured questionnaire, 77
subcultural learning theory, 9, 11–13, 29–30; differential association, 12; incompatibility with Durkheim's anomie, 13–14; strain theory, 12–13. *see also* anomie; social disorganization

theory
sudden wealth. *see* wealth-aspiration
suicide study, of Durkheim, 10, 15, 19–21
Sutherland, Edwin, 12

T
television, 2, 3, 24

V
validity, 115, 116
violence against women, 49, 50
Vold, George B., 12

W
wealth-aspiration, 20, 26, 55–57;
　anomie patterns of, 55–57;
　dependent variables, 84t;
　independent variables, 83–84;
　reliability of scales/indices, 88t
Wilf, Zygi, 121
Wright, John Paul, 16

Y
Yaeger, Don, 5

About the Author

Eric Carter is an assistant professor of sociology at Georgetown College, where he is working on research in the areas of sport and ethics, sustainability, and community. He obtained his Ph.D. from Kansas State University in 2006. He and his family reside in Georgetown, Kentucky.

www.ingramcontent.com/pod-product-compliance
Lightning Source LLC
Chambersburg PA
CBHW021409290426
44108CB00010B/455